OP 22

The US Army on the Mexican Border: A Historical Perspective

Matt M. Matthews

Combat Studies Institute Press
Fort Leavenworth, Kansas

Library of Congress Cataloging-in-Publication Data

Matthews, Matt, 1959-
  The U.S. Army on the Mexican border : a historical perspective / by Matt M. Matthews.
        p. cm. -- (Long war series occasional paper ; 22)
  Includes bibliographical references.
  1. Mexican-American Border Region--History, Military. 2. Mexican-American Border Region--History. 3. United States. Army--History. 4. Geopolitics--United States--History. 5. Geopolitics--Mexico--History. 6. Intervention (International law) 7. National security--United States--History. 8. Border patrols--United States. 9. United States--Foreign relations--Mexico. 10. Mexico--Foreign relations--United States. I. Title. II. Series.

  F786.M44 2007
  355.00972'1--dc22

                                        2007027330

For sale by the Superintendent of Documents, U.S. Government Printing Office
Internet: bookstore.gpo.gov Phone: toll free (866) 512-1800; DC area (202) 512-1800
Fax: (202) 512-2104 Mail: Stop IDCC, Washington, DC 20402-0001

ISBN 978-0-16-078903-8

Foreword

Since the mid-19th century, the United States has frequently employed the US Army on its southern border to perform various roles in support of the Nation—from outright war, to patrolling the border, to chasing bandits while securing persons and property on both sides of the border, and most recently to supporting civil law enforcement and antidrug efforts. Events since 9/11, such as the recent deployment of National Guard Soldiers to the Mexican border, are only the latest manifestation of this long tradition. This 22nd Occasional Paper in the Combat Studies Institute (CSI) Long War Series, *The US Army on the Mexican Border: A Historical Perspective*, by CSI historian Matt M. Matthews, reviews the lengthy history of the US Army on the Mexican border and highlights recurring themes that are relevant to today's ongoing border security mission.

Between 1846 and the early decades of the 20th century, the US Army carried out its security missions under a variety of hardships imposed by the massive length and ruggedness of the border. The shortage of soldiers to police the new and oft-disputed border also proved especially problematic. Mexican domestic politics and US-Mexican international relations greatly affected the Army's operations. Since the 1920s, the Army's role has been dramatically different, ranging from noninvolvement to varied forms of support to local, state, and Federal civilian agencies. Mr. Matthews' narrative brings to light these complexities and makes for compelling reading.

The ongoing, post-9/11 debate over the military's role in securing our Nation's southern border makes this paper important reading for today's Soldiers. While current and future missions will not mirror those of the past, the historical record is replete with insights and lessons learned from the Army's past that are timely and relevant today. *CSI—The Past Is Prologue!*

Timothy R. Reese
Colonel, Armor
Director, Combat Studies Institute

Contents

Maps

Introduction

> I have the honor to inform you, that I have arrived on
> the Line as near as has been ascertained that divides the
> two States of North America and that of Mexico, with two
> hundred Troops of the U.S. Army.
>
> Brevet Major Bennet Riley to his Excellency the
> Governor of Santa Fe, 10 July 1829

On 25 January 1825, US Senator Thomas Hart Benton of Missouri rose on the floor of the Senate to speak in favor of a bill that would mark a road "from the frontier of Missouri to the confines of New Mexico." Missouri traders had been using this road, known as the Santa Fe Trail, to move their caravans of goods from western Missouri to Santa Fe, New Mexico, since 1821. Benton told his fellow senators, "To the people of the West, I know this trade to be an object of the greatest value. . . . The Mexicans are their neighbors, and the only foreign power with whom they can trade."[1] In fact, since gaining independence from Spain in 1821, Mexico, too, had promoted a strong trade relationship between its remote provinces in the north and the frontier states of the American West. By 1825, the newly federalized Republic of Mexico[2] and the United States considered an over-land trade route to be mutually beneficial.

The bill to survey the Santa Fe Trail was signed into law by President James Monroe on 3 March 1825. The new law stipulated that the road would be marked from western Missouri to the Arkansas River. Since the signing of the Transcontinental Treaty[3] with Spain in 1819, the western portion of the Arkansas River constituted a portion of the boundary line between Mexico and the United States (see map 1). The new law also authorized commissioners to make treaties with the various Indian tribes along the trail and to conduct negotiations with the Mexican Government for marking the trail to Santa Fe, New Mexico. Senator Benton was certain the new trail would become "a highway between nations."[4]

In the spring of 1829, at the behest of President Andrew Jackson, the US Army ordered a small contingent of soldiers to move from Jefferson Barracks to Cantonment Leavenworth to begin providing security for the Missouri traders making the dangerous trek to and from Santa Fe, New Mexico. The assignment fell to Brevet Major Bennet Riley and four companies of the 6th Regiment, US Infantry. While a mounted force would certainly have been preferable, at that time the US Army contained only 6,332 soldiers, and the cavalry arm was nonexistent.[5] On 18 April, Brigadier

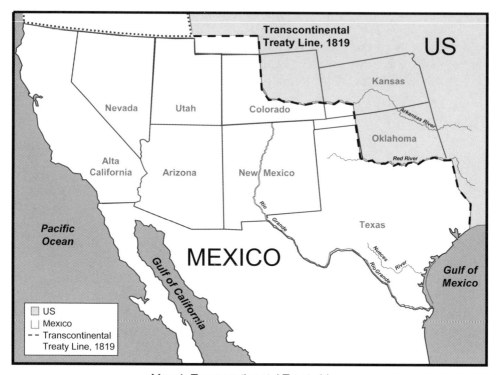

Map 1. Transcontinental Treaty Line.

General Henry Atkinson, Commander of the Western Department, issued the following order:

> Notice is hereby given, that a detachment of two hundred troops, under the command of Maj. [Bennct] Rilcy, of the 6th Regt. Infy., will proceed from Cantonment Leavenworth, about the first of June, on the Santa Fe road, to the Arkansas [R]iver, for the protection of caravans engaged in commercial intercourse with the provinces of New Mexico.
>
> The detachment will halt at some position on the Arkansas, for the return of the caravans, till some time in October, when it will fall back to the frontier.[6]

On 11 June, the US Army contingent linked up with 79 Missouri traders and 38 wagons at Round Grove. On 9 July, Riley's command arrived near Chouteau's Island[7] (located near present-day Lakin, Kansas), a location he considered to be on the border between the United States and

Mexico. From Cantonment Leavenworth, the total distance marched was approximately 400 miles.

Eager to continue on to Santa Fe, the traders crossed the Arkansas River the following day. Before leaving, however, the leader of the caravan, Charles Bent, delivered a letter to Riley in which he expressed the traders' "sincere regret that you are not permitted to accompany us farther yet under the assurance that if danger threatens you will at all times be ready to march to our defence we rest comparatively secure." On the morning of 11 July, Riley crossed to the south side of the Arkansas River to deliver a letter to Bent, which he was to carry to the Governor of Santa Fe:

> I have the honor to inform you, that I have arrived on the Line as near as has been ascertained that divides the two States of North America and that of Mexico, with two hundred Troops of the U.S. Army. The object for which I was sent is the protection of the trade from our Country, to the State over which you Preside, it is hoped therefore that your excellency will feel an equal interest with the United States, and give it all the protection and assistance in your power whilst in your territory, and if possible to send an escort for the protection of the different companies of Traders to the lines as above mentioned or take some suitable means, to prevent Indian depredations. They inform me that the Savages have heretofore been very outrageous on both sides of the Line, and my Government have determined to protect it on their side—I hope therefore that the Trade is of such importance to Mexico that will induce your excellency to adopt a similar course. I shall remain in or about this place until the return of the Company of Traders that are the bearers of this Communication when I should be very glad to see some of the Officers and Soldiers of your excellencies Government.[8]

With Riley's letter in hand, the traders started their long unescorted journey to Santa Fe. Riley assured the traders he would wait until 10 October for their return.

It did not take long for the Missouri traders to run into trouble. Six miles south of the Arkansas, Bent's caravan was attacked by hundreds of Kiowa Indians. A quick counterattack by Bent and the firing of a small cannon saved the caravan from complete annihilation. Terrified by the cannon fire, the Kiowa warriors fell back into an overwatch position in the surrounding hills. Bent quickly ordered his men to dig in and sent riders racing back to the Arkansas to request aid from Riley and his men.[9]

When the riders arrived at 1830 with news of the situation, Riley decided without hesitation to rescue the caravan. That night, Riley and the men of the 6th Infantry Regiment crossed the Arkansas into Mexico, marking the first but certainly not the last time a US Army incursion into Mexican territory would be warranted. At 2300, Riley and his soldiers arrived at Bent's defensive position. The next morning, finding the Indians gone, the caravan began moving south. Riley escorted the traders for 2 days and then returned to the Arkansas where the soldiers awaited its return.[10]

For nearly 3 months, Riley and the soldiers of the 6th Infantry waited for the return of the traders. On the morning of 11 October, Riley gave the command for the firing of the signal gun and ordered his four companies to begin the long journey back to Cantonment Leavenworth. Three miles into their march home, Riley and his small command were overtaken by fast-riding traders. They announced that the caravan was rapidly approaching the Arkansas River with almost 300 people and a large herd of livestock. Traveling with the caravan were approximately 90 traders, a Spanish family, and close to a dozen Spaniards recently exiled from Mexico. To Riley's great relief, the entire procession was guarded by a large contingent of Mexican soldiers under the command of Colonel Jose Antonio Viscarra. Riley recalled:

> I ordered a halt, pitched my tents, and waited for their arrival, which was on the next day, the 12th. When the Col. got nearly across the river, I had my line formed parallel to it, and received him with presented arms. . . . After he had passed, I dismissed the battalion, and received and welcomed him to the territory of the United States; and invited him and the Secretary of the State of Santa Fe to my tent, where we exchanged civilities.[11]

At some point during the official festivities, the Mexican dignitaries handed Major Riley a letter from New Mexico Governor Jose Ano Chavez, in which he stated he had "arranged with . . . Viscarra to help the merchants of North America in their departure from this territory." He also informed Riley that he placed "himself completely" at the major's disposal. On 13 July, both Riley and Viscarra headed for home. "Not without mutual professions of friendship," Riley reported, "and hopes of seeing each other in the Spanish country next year."[12]

The meeting between the US Army and the Mexican Army on the Arkansas River was dignified and cordial and certainly did not reveal any hidden animosity between the two nations. Although Riley had been forced to make a limited incursion into Mexican territory to rescue the traders, the Mexican Government issued no complaint. In the end, Riley was convinced that the entire caravan "would have been destroyed and the people killed if it had not been for the Mexican escort."[13] The encounter between Riley and Viscarra temporarily ushered in a spirit of goodwill between the two republics.

In May 2006, President George W. Bush announced plans to mobilize more than 6,000 Army National Guard Soldiers to assist the Border Patrol in its efforts to secure the US border with Mexico. Now, 177 years after Riley's mission, concerns over possible terrorist infiltration, increasing criminal drug activity, and an alarming influx of illegal immigrants to the United States by way of Mexico have again called for the deployment of US troops to the border. Despite the apparent need for better policing, the announcement was not met with unanimous approval. As history has shown, deployment of US soldiers to the border is often controversial, and the use of military personnel to support law enforcement is at best contentious.

Since the US seizure of half of the Mexican territory during the war with Mexico, the two countries have experienced an ambivalent relationship regarding their shared border. Years of cross-border raids by Indians, bandits, and revolutionaries added to the enmity. Historically, the difficulties were compounded by a growing ethnic disdain on both sides and by the continual instability of the Mexican Government. In this climate of unrest, it is not surprising that the US Army has played a major role in policing the border.

This occasional paper is a concise overview of the history of the US Army's involvement along the Mexican border and offers a fundamental understanding of problems associated with such a mission. Furthermore, it demonstrates how the historic themes addressed—disapproving public reaction, Mexican governmental instability, and insufficient US military personnel to effectively secure the expansive boundary—are still prevalent today.

Chapter 1 addresses the Texas Revolution, the annexation of Texas, and the resulting diplomatic deterioration between the United States and

Mexico. It also examines the mission of the Army of Observation and Army of Occupation on the Mexican border from 1845 to 1846 and the circumstances that led to the Mexican-American War. This conflict and the resulting treaties defined the border and set the stage for the Army's subsequent missions there. The hostility that emerged during and after the war lingers and complicates the relationship between the two countries to this day.

Chapter 2 examines the first attempts by the US Army to secure the Mexican border. Interestingly, these initial efforts were designed to stop Indian raids into Mexico. The Army's attempts were undermined by an insufficient number of soldiers, which made patrolling the expansive border difficult. Static defensive positions proved likewise ineffective in stopping the influx of raiders. The chapter also explores the role of the Texas Rangers and the US Army in protecting the border as well as problems regarding Army involvement with state and local law enforcement. The burning of Piedras Negras, Mexico, by Texas Ranger Captain James H. Callahan as detailed in this chapter provides an example of the challenges encountered by the US Army when dealing with renegade law enforcement officials and vigilantes. Juan Cortina's war is addressed and underscores the difficulties encountered by the US Army when navigating the explosive racial component innate to the border region. Again, many of these issues still exist today.

In chapter 3, Major General Philip H. Sheridan's border campaign against the French and the resulting restoration of goodwill between the United States and Mexico are explored. Also addressed are the disposition of US Army forces on the border from 1870 to 1886 and the inherent weakness of limited manpower and passive defenses in stopping cross-border raids. Colonel Ranald S. Mackenzie's 1873 raid into Mexico and Lieutenant Colonel William "Pecos Bill" Shafter's preemptive strikes across the border are also discussed. These cross-border attacks reduced much of the raiding but created a political firestorm that helped erode goodwill between the United States and Mexico.

Chapter 4 investigates US Army dispositions on the border from 1911 to 1917 and the chaos created by the Mexican Revolution. Once again, the US Army found that maintaining mere static defenses and patrolling could not stop terrorist raiders determined to cross the border. Major General Frederick Funston's attempts to stop the Plan of San Diego plotters and Brigadier General John J. Pershing's Punitive Expedition against Francisco "Pancho" Villa are closely examined. In both cases, the US Army was again forced to conduct hot pursuits and preemptive strikes into Mexico to restore order to the border.

The final chapter includes an overview of the US Army on the border from 1919 to 1953 and briefly examines the US Army's response to Operation WETBACK in 1954. Chapter 5's major focus is the increasing military presence on the US-Mexican border from 1978 to the present because of US immigration and drug enforcement polices. Also addressed is the evolution of military support to law enforcement along the southern border.

While modern US Army missions along the Mexican border are a far cry from the chaos and turmoil of the 19th and early 20th centuries, many of the historic problems remain. It is, therefore, important that US Army officers understand the lessons of the past and have a solid grasp of the history and lessons associated with the US Army on the Mexican border.

Notes

1. *Register of Debates in Congress*, 18th Cong., 2nd sess., 1825, 341–344, quoted in Richard O. Ulibarri, *American Interest in the Spanish Southwest, 1803–1848* (San Francisco: R&E Research Associates, 1974), 106.

2. Mexico became a federal republic under its first constitution in 1824. See Lynn V. Foster, *A Brief History of Mexico* (New York: Facts on File, Inc., 1997).

3. By far the best account of the Transcontinental Treaty with Spain can be found in Samuel Flagg Bemis, *John Quincy Adams and the Foundations of American Foreign Policy* (New York: Alfred A. Knopf, 1949).

4. David Dary, *The Santa Fe Trail: Its History, Legends, and Lore* (New York: Alfred A. Knopf, 2000), 92. For a complete history of the diplomacy involved in opening the Santa Fe Trail, see William R. Manning, *Early Diplomatic Relations Between the United States and Mexico* (New York: Greenwood Press Publishers, 1968).

5. Russell F. Weigley, *History of the United States Army* (Bloomington: Indiana University Press, 1984), 596; Otis E. Young, *The First Military Escort on the Santa Fe Trail, 1829, From the Journal and Reports of Major Bennet Riley and Lieutenant Philip St. George Cooke* (Glendale, CA: The Arthur H. Clark Company, 1952), 49.

6. Young, 39–40.

7. Chouteau's Island was named after Auguste P. Chouteau, a hunter and trapper who may have established a trading post on the island. Blue Skyways, Kansas State Library, *Chouteau's Island*, http://skyways.lib.ks.us/history/chouteau. html; Frank W. Blackmar, *Kansas: A Cyclopedia of State History, Embracing Events, Institutions, Industries, Counties, Cites, Towns, Prominent Persons, etc.* (Chicago: Standard Printing Company, 1912), 339–340.

8. Young, 180–182.

9. Ibid., 90–91; "Report of Major Riley," *The New-York Spectator*, 26 February 1830.

10. Young, 95; "Report of Major Riley;" Leo E. Oliva, *Soldiers on the Santa Fe Trail* (Norman: University of Oklahoma Press, 1967), 30.

11. Young, 139–140; "Report of Major Riley."

12. Young, 192–193; "Report of Major Riley."

13. "Report of Major Riley."

Chapter 1

Setting the Stage: The Army of Observation and Army of Occupation on the Mexican Border, 1845–46

At this late day not one-third of the army here could take the field; and for the limited means we have, except such as came with the 2d dragoons, we are indebted to those with whom we are expected to contend—the Mexicans. . . . We occupy the anomalous position of invited guests, paying for our dinners! Great people, those Texans! Annex 'em, by all means!

> Unknown US Army Officer with the
> "Army of Occupation," Letter to the Editor
> of the *N.O. Picayune*, 1 November 1845

Hostilities may now be considered as commenced.

> General Zachary Taylor to President James K. Polk

By what authority, superior to the Constitution, [have we] become involved in War, the beginning of which we now see, but the end of which no man can foretell.

> *The National Intelligencer*, May 1846

For myself, I was bitterly opposed to the measure, and to this day regard the war which resulted as one of the most unjust ever waged by a stronger against a weaker nation. It was an instance of a republic following the bad example of European monarchies, in not considering justice in their desire to acquire additional territory.

> President Ulysses S. Grant

The Texas Revolution

A mere decade after becoming a republic, Mexico's constitutional government was torn apart by General Antonio Lopez de Santa Anna. A self-absorbed opportunist, Santa Anna was portrayed by one keen Mexican observer as a man "'in a state of perpetual agitation' so exalted that his 'soul doesn't fit in his body.'"[1] In 1834, Santa Anna abolished the constitution and declared himself the de facto leader of both the Mexican Government and the Army. By 1835, numerous Mexican states openly challenged the new dictator. In the Mexican province of Texas, heavily populated by Anglos[2] and Tejanos,[3] Santa Anna's actions were met with outright revolt.[4]

The Texans responded to Santa Anna by launching a full-scale assault on Mexican military forces in Texas. In December 1835, after capturing the settlements of Gonzales and Goliad, the small Anglo and Tejano volunteer army captured Santa Anna's brother-in-law and his entire command at San Antonio de Bexar. Elated by their victory, the Texans issued the Declaration of Causes for Taking up Arms Against Mexico and began organizing a new government. Outraged by the stunning turn of events, Santa Anna hastily marched an Army of 6,000 men north into Texas. Confident of an easy victory, the bombastic Mexican dictator informed European dignitaries in Mexico City that, if the US Government were found to be assisting the Texans, "he would continue the march of his army to Washington and place upon its Capital the Mexican Flag."[5]

"The foreigners who waged war against the Mexican nation have violated all laws and do not deserve consideration," Santa Anna told his soldiers. "No quarter will be given them. . . . They have audaciously declared a war of extermination to the Mexicans and should be treated in the same manner."[6] True to his word, the Mexican leader marched his army 1,000 miles north in the middle of winter. Santa Anna arrived in San Antonio with part of his army on 23 February 1836 and laid siege to the Alamo, a former Catholic mission. On the morning of 6 March, after a 13-day siege, Santa Anna and approximately 2,500 Mexican soldiers overran the Alamo's 190 defenders. The Texans, along with American volunteers who survived the fight, were executed after they surrendered. Twenty-one days later, roughly 333 Texans, who had been captured near Goliad on 20 March, were brutally executed on orders from Santa Anna.[7]

While he had certainly been successful thus far, Santa Anna's early victories bred hubris and a total disregard for the fighting qualities of the Texans. As the Mexican commander drove his men farther east into the heart of Texas, the leader of the greatly reduced Texas Army, Major General Samuel P. Houston, continued to retreat. On 21 April 1836, however, Houston stopped running and unleashed his vengeful army on the unsuspecting Mexicans. The greatly outnumbered Texans launched their surprise attack against Santa Anna's forces near the banks of the San Jacinto River and, within hours, killed 630 Mexican soldiers and forced 730 to surrender. In revenge for the atrocities committed at the Alamo and Goliad, the Texans butchered many of their Mexican prisoners.[8]

The following day, Houston's men captured Santa Anna, who had managed to escape from the carnage of San Jacinto. Houston promised to spare Santa Anna's life if the dictator would guarantee to remove all Mexican soldiers from Texas and agree to place them south of the Rio

Grande. Santa Anna agreed and, on 14 May 1836, signed a public version of the Treaty of Velasco as well as a private version. In the latter rendition, Santa Anna promised to lobby the Mexican Government for Texas independence. The Treaty of Velasco also designated the Rio Grande the new border between Texas and Mexico.

In the following months, the Mexican Army displaced south of the Rio Grande, and in 1837, Santa Anna returned to Mexico. On his return, the disgraced leader found Mexico in a state of shock over his defeat. The new conservative government in Mexico refused to endorse the Treaty of Velasco and immediately began planning to march its army back across the Rio Grande. Meanwhile, in Washington, President Andrew Jackson's Administration hastily recognized the new independent Republic of Texas. But all was not settled. The controversy continued to simmer for nearly a decade, at which time the US Army once again was called to the southern border.[9]

Although President Jackson and a host of other southern politicians earnestly pressed for the annexation of Texas, northern antislavery forces were able to temporarily hold them at bay.[10] In Mexico, continued internal strife prevented the Mexican Army from taking immediate action against the Texans. In 1841, however, as the United States and the Republic of Texas continued to debate annexation and statehood, the President of Texas, Mirabeau Bonaparte Lamar, invaded New Mexico, which Texans claimed belonged to them. The invaders were soon captured and dispatched to prison in Mexico City. Reprisals came swiftly as a Mexican raiding party captured San Antonio and apprehended more Texans. The Texans retaliated by launching raids across the Rio Grande. The Mexican Army shot 1 in 10 of the 200 raiders who were captured in Mier, Mexico.[11]

While many Americans bitterly opposed the annexation of Texas, the election of expansionist James K. Polk as President of the United States in 1844 led outgoing President John Tyler to believe he had a mandate to annex the Republic. Continued British meddling in Mexican and Texan affairs forced Tyler to move quickly. Convinced he could never secure a two-thirds majority vote in the Senate, Tyler and other expansionist politicians concocted a simple joint resolution that required a straightforward majority vote. The resolution to annex Texas into the Union passed the House on 25 January 1845 and the Senate on 27 February 1845. On 1 March 1845, President Tyler signed the joint resolution.[12] Mexican Minister General Juan N. Anonte responded less than a week later to the news, informing US Secretary of State John C. Calhoun that he considered the annexation of Texas "an act of aggression, the most unjust which can be found recorded in the annals of modern history."[13]

The Army of Observation

On 28 May 1845, Secretary of War William L. Marcy wrote to Brigadier General Zachary Taylor, Commander of US Army forces at Fort Jesup, Louisiana, alerting the general of the possibility of moving his forces into Texas.

> So soon as the Texas Congress shall have given its consent to annexation, and a convention shall assemble and accept the terms offered in the resolution of Congress, Texas will then be regarded by the executive government here so far a part of the United States as to be entitled . . . to defense and protection from foreign invasion and Indian incursions. The troops under your command will be placed and kept in readiness to perform that duty.[14]

Taylor, a 60-year-old Army veteran, had been sent to Fort Jesup in June 1844 in anticipation of annexation. As the Commander of the 1st Military Department, Taylor, along with the 1,200 soldiers under his command, waited for more than a year at the fort and outlying camps for politicians in Washington to make a decision. Taylor's forces were aptly named "The Army of Observation."[15]

On 29 June 1845, Taylor's long wait ended. Anticipating Texas ratification of the annexation resolution, acting Secretary of War George Bancroft (temporarily filling in for Marcy), under orders from President Polk, ordered Taylor to move his Army of Observation into Texas "on or near the Rio Grande." Polk, deeply concerned that Texas ratification would lead to a Mexican military response, ordered Taylor to locate "a site as will consist with the health of the troops, and will be best adapted to repel invasion, and to protect what, in the event of annexation, will be our [south] western border."[16] The President also ordered a naval squadron into position off the shore of Veracruz, Mexico, and dispatched another naval squadron to the shores of California. At this time, Polk was adamant that Taylor not trigger a war between the United States and Mexico. The situation was exacerbated because no one had a firm grasp on where the Mexican border would actually be located after ratification.[17] As historian Holman Hamilton points out, "The title to the region between the Nueces and the Rio Grande was obscured in a half century of controversy. Neither Polk nor Taylor possessed accurate information on the topography of the land south of Corpus Christi [Texas]."[18] These concerns were articulated by Marcy in a more detailed order to Taylor dated 8 July:

> This department is informed that Mexico has some military establishments on the east side of the Rio Grande,

which are, and for some time have been in the actual occupancy of her troops. In carrying out the instructions heretofore received, you will be careful to avoid any acts of aggression unless an actual state of war should exist. The Mexican forces at the post in their possession, and which have been so, will not be disturbed as long as the relations of peace between the United States and Mexico continue.[19]

While certainly not a brilliant military officer, Taylor was endowed with a strong measure of common sense. He had decided well before Marcy's order to advance his Army to Corpus Christi, located at the mouth of the Nueces.[20] Taylor moved his infantry to New Orleans, sending them by ship to Corpus Christi, while his cavalry marched south to the new location. By August 1845, Taylor had assembled his newly designated "Army of Occupation" at Corpus Christi.

The US Army of Occupation

By most accounts, the living conditions for the Army of Occupation at Corpus Christi were dismal. Disease and sickness were rampant.[21] The War Department, however, continued to send Regular Army soldiers to Corpus Christi, and by the middle of October 1845, nearly 4,000 men were assembled in the miserable encampment. According to historian K. Jack Bauer, "This represented approximately half the total strength of the army and was the largest force assembled since the War of 1812."[22] While politicians in Washington continued to search for a peaceful political solution to the crisis, the Adjutant General of the Army informed Taylor that, "although a state of war with Mexico, or an invasion of Texas by her forces, may not take place, it is . . . proper and necessary that your forces shall be fully equal to meet with certainty of success any crisis which may arise in Texas and which would require you by force of arms to carry out the instructions of the Government."[23] With this in mind, Taylor's Army began an intense training regimen designed to provide the Army of Occupation a rudimentary exposure to drilling and maneuvering battalions, regiments, and brigade-size units.

With the approach of winter, training came to an abrupt halt. Bad weather and Taylor's lack of interest in continued drilling caused many problems. With the bitter cold came increased sickness and with little to occupy their time, many soldiers began committing all manner of depredations against the local Mexican population. The problem became so acute that Taylor was forced to confine his soldiers to camp during the night.

Writing to his hometown newspaper, one disgruntled officer summed up his thoughts on the campaign:

> The blundering manner in which this Texas campaign had been conducted by the authorities at Washington is infinitely disgraceful to all concerned. Most fortunate it was for the lives, as well as the reputation, of the U.S. Troops dispatched to Corpus Christi in such hot haste, that they found no enemy to oppose their landing. Had it been any other power than Mexico, with whom we were seeking a quarrel, our 'army of occupation' would have been cut up in detail.[24]

In November, President Polk dispatched Louisiana Congressman John Slidell to Mexico to hammer out some sort of agreement with the Mexican Government. Slidell's arrival in Veracruz, Mexico, ignited a firestorm of controversy. Mexican President Jose Joaquin de Herrera refused to meet with Slidell, and the Mexican Government refused to accept his credentials. Herrera, long suspected by many Mexicans as an appeaser, was castigated for his lack of aggressive action against the Americans.[25] With public support wavering for Herrera, General Mariano Paredes y Arrillaga launched a coup, driving Herrera from power. By January 1846, Paredes assumed the mantle of the Mexican presidency. He soon proved determined to offer a more aggressive stance against the Americans, swearing to his people he would take back Texas.[26]

Taylor's March to the Rio Grande

President Polk was determined to take a more combative position toward the Mexican Government. When he received word that Congressman Slidell's efforts to meet with Herrera had been soundly rejected, Polk immediately decided to ratchet up pressure on Mexico by ordering Taylor to march his Army to the Rio Grande. On 13 January 1846, Secretary of War Marcy sent the following order to Taylor:

> I am directed by the President to instruct you to advance and occupy, with the troops under your command, positions on or near the east bank of the Rio del Norte as soon as it can be conveniently done with reference to the season and the routes by which your movements must be made. From the views heretofore presented to this department, it is presumed Point Isabel will be considered by you an eligible position. This point, or some one near it, and points opposite Matamoros and Mier, and in the vicinity of Laredo, are suggested for your consideration; but you

are left to your better knowledge to determine the post or posts which you are to occupy, as well as the question of dividing your forces with a view to occupying two or more positions.

In the positions you may take in carrying out these instructions and other movements that may be made, the use of the Rio del Norte may be very convenient if not necessary. Should you attempt to exercise the right which the United States have in common with Mexico to the free navigation of this river, it is probable that Mexico would interpose resistance. You will not attempt to enforce this right without further instructions. . . .

It is not designed, in our present relations with Mexico, that you should treat her as an enemy; but should she assume that character by a declaration of war, or any open act of hostility towards us, you will not act merely on the defensive if your relative means enable you to do otherwise.

Polk's reasoning in sending Taylor's Army to the Rio Grande has long been debated by historians.[27] It is possible Polk actually believed a peaceful outcome was still possible. It is equally conceivable that the President knew the Mexican Government would never acquiesce to an American Army on the Rio Grande. Without doubt, however, Marcy's order of 13 January placed the United States on a collision course with Mexico.[28]

At the time, public opinion varied on Polk's provocative order. While many Americans enthusiastically supported Polk's expansionist policy, others remained deeply cynical of the President's method. In the months to follow, the newspaper, *The National Intelligencer*, asked Congress "to enquire [sic] why, and for what purposes, this army was marched to the Rio Grande, and there placed in menacing array against the forces of a nation with whom this Government is (or was) at peace, and at the time, engaged in diplomatic intercourse? [sic][29]

Fearful of rainy weather conditions, Taylor waited until March to move his Army to the Rio Grande. Many sick and ailing soldiers were transported by ship to Point Isabel, Texas, along with a company of artillery, siege guns, and various surplus belongings. This location was vital as it served as the primary supply depot for the operation. Taylor planned to move the rest of his Army overland down the "Road of the Arroyo Colorado." The road was actually little more than a dirt footpath running between Matamoros, Mexico, and Corpus Christi. Seriously hampered by a lack of wagons and horses, Taylor's quartermasters were forced to rely on Mexican smugglers and ranchers to help procure the Army's transport. Ultimately, each company was allowed only one wagon to carry its baggage. On 8 March, Colonel David E. Twiggs, commanding Taylor's advance guard, marched out of Corpus Christi with the 2d Dragoon Regiment and Brevet Major Samuel Ringgold's light artillery. For the next 3 days, Brevet Brigadier General William J. Worth's 1st Brigade, Colonel James S. McIntosh's 2d Brigade, and Colonel William Whistler's 3d Brigade left Corpus Christi and began a 150-mile trek to the Rio Grande.[30] Before leaving Corpus Christi, Taylor issued the following order to his troops:

> The army of occupation of Texas being now about to take a position upon the left bank of the Rio Grande, under the orders of the Executive of the United States, the general-in-chief desires to express the hope that the movement will be advantageous to all concerned; and with the object of attaining this laudable end, he has ordered all under his command to observe, with the most scrupulous respect, the rights of all the inhabitants who may be found in peaceful prosecution of their respective occupations, as well on the left as on the right side of the Rio Grande. Under no pretext, nor in any way, will any interference be allowed with the civil rights or religious privileges of the inhabitants; but the utmost respect for them will be maintained.[31]

Many Americans remained uncertain of the rightful ownership of the land between the Nueces and the Rio Grande. Taylor, however, was undeterred and boldly advanced his Army into a strip of land the Mexicans steadfastly claimed as their own. Remarkably, he did so with only slightly more than 3,500 men. While the advocates of Manifest Destiny were hopeful of a peaceful outcome, Taylor's encounter with the Mexicans on the Rio Grande proved to be a far cry from Bennet Riley's experience on the Arkansas in 1829.

The first signs of trouble for Taylor's Army came on 14 March. On that day, Twiggs's cavalry contingent observed a small group of Mexicans setting fire to the prairie grass. On 15 March, Mexican Lieutenant Ramon Falcon met a small advance party of US cavalry troops and advised them not to advance any farther as the Mexican Army was prepared to resist. About 30 miles from the Rio Grande, on the north side of the Arroyo Colorado, Taylor consolidated his forces. Concerned that the Mexican Army would oppose his crossing, he prepared for an assault. Captain Jose Barragan, a staff officer for General Francisco de Mejia, the Garrison Commander of Matamoros, delivered a message to Taylor from Mejia on 20 March. The proclamation called on Mexican citizens to rise up against "the degenerate sons of Washington." Barragan furthermore informed Taylor that the Mexican Army would oppose his crossing of the Arroyo Colorado and that any crossing would be considered an act of war. Sweeping aside the Mexican protest, Taylor announced, "We will cross immediately and if a single man of you shows his face after my men enter the river, I will open an artillery fire on him."[32]

At 0930, Taylor's Army crossed the Arroyo without a shot being fired. As the US infantry splashed into the water, the Mexican cavalry beat a hasty retreat to Matamoros. General Mejia, lacking orders from his superiors, had forbidden his men to attack the Americans. For the moment, bluffing the US Army appeared to be his only option. Unbeknown to Taylor, the Mexican garrison at Matamoros was still awaiting 2,000 reinforcements from President Paredes. Like the rest of Mexico's 20,000-man army, Mejia's contingent was ill-prepared for war. According to historians David and Jeanne Heidler, the Mexican Army at the time was "a scattered, badly disciplined, disaffected rabble with little motivation for fighting anyone, especially Americans."[33]

On 28 March, Taylor's Army reached the north bank of the Rio Grande, opposite the town of Matamoros, and immediately raised the American flag. As Mexicans crowded onto rooftops in Matamoros to watch, Taylor dispatched General Worth to the south side of the river to confer with Mejia. The Mexican general refused to talk with Worth but did send Brigadier General Romulo Diaz de la Vega to consult with the American officer. Since no one in Worth's party understood Spanish and no one in Vega's command could converse in English, French was used to break the language barrier. Worth informed Vega that the US Army's move to the Rio Grande should not be construed as an antagonistic act or an assault on Mexico. While Vega agreed that the two countries were not at war, Worth received a decidedly cool reception.[34] An American officer writing to *The Cleveland Herald* stated:

> The Mexicans over the river are very angry, and will have nothing to say to us. Gen. Worth went over this afternoon, but they would not let him enter the town, nor would General Mejia come out to receive him, sending one of his officers. General Worth took over a dispatch from Taylor, but as General Mejia would not see him, he brought it back. General Mejia says he will only condescend to see

General Taylor himself. In a few days we expect to come to a better understanding.[35]

Still awaiting reinforcements, Mejia could do little more than improve his fortifications around Matamoros. Fearful of a possible Mexican offensive, Taylor began constructing his own fort on the north bank of the Rio Grande. The new fortification, christened Fort Texas, was erected with walls 9 feet high and 15 feet thick. It was designed to hold 800 men. The batteries placed inside were aimed directly at Matamoros.[36]

For the next few days, Taylor convinced Mejia to return two US Army dragoons the Mexicans had detained. Hoping, even at this late date, to avert war, Taylor advised his soldiers to observe "proper courtesy and dignity in their intercourse with the inhabitants . . . [since] our attitude is essentially pacific and our policy conciliatory."[37] While Taylor's Army remained encamped on the Rio Grande, approximately 200 American soldiers and 6 slaves took the harmonious policy to the extreme, swimming the river and deserting to the Mexicans. Many of these soldiers were immigrants and were enticed by Mexican offers of free land.[38]

Scores of soldiers with Taylor's Army were vehemently opposed to President Polk's brash policy toward the Mexicans. Like many Americans, Colonel Ethan Hitchcock, Commander of the 3d Infantry Regiment, questioned the entire premise of Taylor's operations on the Rio Grande. "We have not one particle of right to be here," he wrote. "Our force is altogether too small for the accomplishment of its errand. It looks as if the government sent a small force on purpose to bring on war, so to have a pretext for taking California and as much of this country as it chooses."[39] Lieutenant Ulysses S. Grant later recollected that the Army's advance to the Rio Grande was conducted "apparently in order to force Mexico to initiate war."[40] All too soon, Hitchcock's and Grant's assessments proved extraordinarily prophetic.

On 10 April, Taylor's quartermaster, Colonel Trueman Cross, failed to return after a horse-riding excursion. A patrol sent to look for Cross was ambushed, resulting in the death of Lieutenant David Porter. Cross's body was found later, the apparent victim of a robbery. Historian K. Jack Bauer was certain that "the two incidents added to the tension between the two armies, since there lingered in American minds a belief of official Mexican complicity in the deaths. In all probability there was none."[41]

General Pedro de Ampudia arrived in Matamoros on 11 April to replace Mejia. Three days behind him and marching rapidly toward Matamoros were 2,000 additional soldiers. Without President Paredes's approval,

Ampudia planned to attack the Americans on the 15th and promptly sent an ultimatum to Taylor:

> To Don Z. Taylor: . . . I require you in all form, and at the latest in the peremptory term of twenty-four hours, to break up your camp and return to the east bank of the Nueces River while our Governments are regulating the pending question in relation to Texas. If you insist on remaining upon the soil of the Department of Tamaulipas, it will certainly result that arms, and arms alone, must decide the question; and in that case I advise you that we accept the war to which, with so much injustice on your part, you provoke us. . . .[42]

Taylor was not at all impressed by Ampudia's bravado. "I regret the alternative which you offer," he responded, "but at the same time, wish it understood that I shall by no means avoid such alternative."[43] Believing war was imminent, Taylor ordered US Navy ships to seal off the entrance to the Rio Grande. According to John S. D. Eisenhower, "The American naval commander at Brazos Santiago was to stop all vessels and remove all munitions of war and food bound for Matamoros. With six thousand Mexican troops in that city, rations would soon be short and the Mexican command would be forced to act."[44] Ampudia's plan to attack the Americans on the 15th failed to materialize when his subordinates refused to sanction his plan without orders from Paredes.[45]

The situation on the Rio Grande changed drastically on 24 April with the arrival of General Mariano Arista in Matamoros. Paredes's Minister of War, General Jose Maria Tornel, had dispatched Arista to replace Ampudia as the Commander of the Division of the North. Arista had received orders from Tornel on 4 April to attack the Americans. At the same time, Tornel had ordered Ampudia to take no action against the Americans until Arista arrived with reinforcements. Arista wasted little time in carrying out his orders. In fact, the day before arriving in Matamoros, he ordered Brigadier General Anastasio Torrejon and 1,600 cavalry troopers to cross the Rio Grande 14 miles upstream from Fort Texas and move on Point Isabel to cut Taylor off from his base of supply. Arista also hoped to draw Taylor out of his fortifications. On entering Matamoros on the 24th, Arista informed Taylor that hostilities had commenced.[46] (Map 2 shows Taylor's Army on the Rio Grande.)

At first, Taylor, believed a large Mexican force had crossed the Rio Grande downstream from Fort Texas and sent a party of dragoons east to reconnoiter possible crossing sites. That night, however, he received new

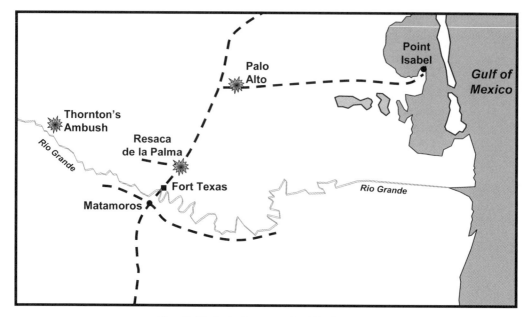

Map 2. Taylor's Army on the Rio Grande.

intelligence that indicated that a large force had crossed the Rio Grande upstream from his location. Taylor responded to this second report by dispatching Captain Seth B. Thornton and two squadrons of dragoons. Riding 25 miles upriver, Thornton and 63 of his dragoons arrived at Rancho de Carricitos on the morning of 25 April. Unbeknown to Thornton, he had ridden into a cleverly concealed ambush site. The clash was swift and brutal. By the time it ended, Torrejon's mounted troopers had killed 14 and captured 50 dragoons.

When reports of the clash reached Taylor on the 26th, he immediately informed Washington:

> I have respectfully to report that General Arista arrived in Matamoros on the 24th instant and assumed the chief command of the Mexican troops. . . . I regret to report that a party of dragoons sent out by me on the 24th instant to watch the course of the river above this bank became engaged with a very large force of the enemy, and after a short affair in which sixteen were killed and wounded, [the party] appears to have been surrounded and compelled to surrender. Not one in the party has returned, except a wounded man sent in this morning by the Mexican commander, so that I cannot report with confidence the

particulars of the engagement or the fate of the officers. . . . Hostilities may now be considered as commenced. . . .[47]

Taylor also asked Polk for volunteers from Louisiana to help reinforce his small Regular Army contingent.

Taylor was certain Torrejon was attempting to capture his supply base at Point Isabel, and so, leaving a mere 500 men at Fort Texas, he began moving the rest of his command north. Arista had hoped Torrejon's flanking movement would cause Taylor to pull back from the Rio Grande. When he learned that most of the American Army was marching toward Point Isabel, Arista moved his soldiers across the river. Leaving Ampudia to besiege Fort Texas with 1,200 men, Arista moved into a blocking position at Palo Alto to prevent Taylor from liberating his encircled soldiers at Fort Texas.[48]

After securing Point Isabel, Taylor marched his 2,500-man Army south and, on 8 May, engaged Arista's 3,300 soldiers at Palo Alto. In the bloody contest that ensued, Taylor's Army stood its ground and beat back flanking attempts by the Mexican cavalry with the aid of Major Samuel Ringgold's newly developed "flying artillery."[49] By the time night fell, Arista had had enough and withdrew his forces south to a dry creek bed called Resaca del la Palma. The next day, Taylor followed Arista to his new defensive position. Although the Mexican forces occupied an advantageous position, Taylor launched an immediate assault. After taking grievous losses and losing an artillery battery, the Mexican line broke. As Arista's men attempted to make their way across the Rio Grande to safety, many drowned or were shot by the pursuing Americans as they tried to swim to the opposite bank.

In Fort Texas, the jubilant defenders watched the Mexicans run past and applauded the near annihilation of Arista's army. In the 2 days of fighting, 34 of Taylor's men were killed, and 113 suffered wounds. Lieutenant George G. Meade, an engineering officer under Taylor who later commanded the Army of the Potomac at Gettysburg, reported 1,200 dead and wounded Mexicans, 300 of whom drowned in the Rio Grande. Meade also estimated that 1,000 to 2,000 Mexican soldiers deserted.[50] As the bloated corpses of Mexican soldiers floated downstream, President Polk prepared to begin the war in earnest.

Armed with the news of the Thornton ambush, yet still unaware of Taylor's victory, Polk submitted his war message to Congress on 11 May. In a debate reminiscent of today's political discourse, expansionists presented their agenda. "The fear of the people," Polk acknowledged, would force Congress to declare war. Polk and his surrogates attached the declaration of war to an emergency resupply for Taylor's Army, knowing full well that a vote against war would appear as a vote against Taylor's besieged forces. According to historians David and Jeanne Heidler, "Polk raised the specter that Taylor and his men were in great peril before overwhelming Mexican forces that could have already destroyed them, and he requested $10 million and authorization to raise fifty thousand volunteers."[51] While many remained skeptical, both the House and the Senate passed the measure into law by wide margins. One of the few Congressmen to vote against the declaration of war was former President John Quincy Adams. According to historian Paul C. Nagel, Adams viewed the vote as "the greatest sin yet committed by the slavemongers as they sought to enlarge their domain."[52] By the time the Mexican War ended, the promoters of Manifest Destiny had achieved their goal of a nation stretching from the Atlantic to the Pacific. In so doing, however, a schism was forged between the United States and Mexico that many argue exists to this day.

A scant 16 months after Taylor's Army of Occupation chased the Mexican Army back across the Rio Grande, Major General Winfield Scott led US forces into the Mexican capital. During the entire bloody campaign, the Mexicans had failed to win a single battle. By February 1848, Mexican President Manuel de la Pena y Pena conceded defeat and signed the Treaty of Guadalupe Hidalgo. The treaty forced Mexico to relinquish control of Alta California and New Mexico and to give up all claims to Texas. The agreement also fixed the Rio Grande as the explicit boundary between Texas and Mexico. In exchange for losing almost half its country, the United States agreed to pay the Mexican Government $15 million and to assume any debt Mexico owed to US citizens. Remarkably, the vote to authorize the treaty passed the US Senate with three votes to spare. Many of the dissenting votes were cast by Senators who wanted the United States to seize all of Mexico, while other politicians believed the entire affair an absolute swindle.[53]

In the end, according to historian T. R. Fehrenbach, the war "reduced Mexico permanently to second place upon the continent. This is what was so bitterly felt by the politicized Mexicans, who considered themselves rivals of the North Americans and culturally their superiors. . . . The Intervention ended in a profound sense of loss of dignity and self-respect, laced with fears for the future of the country and a lasting phobia toward all 'interventions.'"[54] In 1853, the United States paid Mexico $10 million for another sizable piece of land bordering northwest Mexico and New Mexico. Known as the Gadsden Purchase, this acquisition marked the last transfer of territory by Mexico to the United States.[55]

Notes

1.   Carol Christensen and Thomas Christensen, *The U.S-Mexican War* (San Francisco: Bay Books, 1998), 22; Edward H. Moseley and Paul C. Clark Jr., *Historical Dictionary of the United States-Mexican War* (Lanham, MD, and London: The Scarecrow Press, Inc., 1997), 245.

2.   The word generally refers to white English-speaking Americans.

3.   Refers to Mexican-Texans born in Texas.

4.   Christensen and Christensen, 23; David S. Heidler and Jeanne T. Heidler, *The Mexican War* (Westport, CT: Greenwood Press, 2006), 34–35.

5.   Wilfrid Hardy Callcott, *Santa Anna: The Story of an Enigma Who Once Was Mexico* (Norman: University of Oklahoma Press, 1936), 125–126.

6.   Christensen and Christensen, 25.

7.   Albert A. Nofi, *The Alamo and the Texas War for Independence* (New York: De Capo, 1994), 107–108; Christensen and Christensen, 25; Richard Bruce Winders, *Crisis in the Southwest: The United States, Mexico, and the Struggle Over Texas* (Wilmington, DE: SR Books, 2002), 23–24.

8.   Nofi, 149–159; Winders, 27. Historian Sam W. Haynes called the Battle of San Jacinto a "war atrocity in its own right." Christensen and Christensen, 26.

9.   Lynn V. Foster, *A Brief History of Mexico* (New York: Facts on File, 1997), 120; Winders, 34; Daniel James, *Mexico and the Americans* (New York: Frederick A. Praeger, 1963), 58–59.

10.   Winders, 81.

11.   Ibid., 30–70.

12.   David Heidler and Jeanne Heidler wrote that "the annexation resolution sailed through the expansionist house on January 25, 1845, by a comfortable vote of 120 to 98, but it barely squeaked through the bitterly divided Senate on February 27, 1845, by a margin of two votes (27 to 25). Regardless of the mixed nature of the vote, the matter was done. . . . The apparent disregard of constitutional protocol to satisfy expansionist expediency infuriated abolitionists, but their voices could not carry in the heady atmosphere of Manifest Destiny." Heidler and Heidler, 44–45.

13.   K. Jack Bauer, *The Mexican War, 1846–1848* (New York: Macmillan Publishing Company, 1974), 16.

14.   Holman Hamilton, *Zachary Taylor: Soldier of the Republic* (Indianapolis, IN: The Bobbs-Merrill Company, 1941), 159.

15.   Ibid., 157–158; Winders, 92.

16.   David M. Pletcher, *The Diplomacy of Annexation: Texas, Oregon, and the Mexican War* (Columbia: University of Missouri Press, 1973), 255.

17.   Hamilton, 159, 162; Winders, 92.

18.   Hamilton, 162.

19.   Ward McAfee and J. Cordell Robinson, *Origins of the Mexican War: A Documentary Source Book*, vol. 1, *U.S. Relations With Latin American Nations* (Salisbury NC: Documentary Publications, 1982), 16.

20. According to Russell F. Weigley, "Zachary Taylor's forte was battlefield command, not administration or staff work." Russell F. Weigley, *History of the United States Army* (Bloomington: Indiana University Press, 1984), 181.

21. Paul Foos, *A Short Offhand Killing Affair: Soldiers and Social Conflict During the Mexican-American War* (Chapel Hill: The University of North Carolina Press, 2002), 17–18.

22. Bauer, 33.

23. Ibid., 32–33.

24. Ibid., 34; "Army of Occupation," *Milwaukie Daily Sentinel,* 6 December 1845.

25. Pletcher, 353–354.

26. Winders, 94–95; John S. D. Eisenhower, *So Far From God: The U.S. War With Mexico, 1846–1848* (New York: Random House, 1989), 46–47; Heidler and Heidler, 59.

27. Richard Bruce Winders wrote: "In the wake of the Mexican defeat at the Battle of San Jacinto, officials of the new Texas government established a precedent for designating the Rio Grande as the border of the new republic by insisting in the Treaty of Velasco that the area north of the river be free of any Mexican troops. In December that same year the Republic of Texas Congress officially adopted the Rio Grande as its southern and western boundary. Even though Mexico had been able to defend its claim to New Mexico and had temporarily reoccupied such towns as San Antonio and Goliad in 1842, in private circles many Mexicans admitted that Texas, including the disputed territory, was lost." Winders, 94.

28. McAfee and Robinson, 5; Eisenhower, 49–50.

29. *The National Intelligencer* quoted in *The Cleveland Herald,* 15 May 1846.

30. Hamilton, 171; Eisenhower, 51; Bauer, 37–38.

31. Hamilton, 173.

32. Bauer, 38–39; Heidler and Heidler, 58; Hamilton, 173.

33. Heidler and Heidler, 59.

34. Bauer, 40.

35. *The Cleveland Herald,* 22 April 1846.

36. Anton Adams, *The War in Mexico* (Chicago: The Emperor's Press, 1998), 19.

37. Bauer, 41.

38. Ibid., 41–42; Eisenhower, 62.

39. Pletcher, 376.

40. U. S. Grant, *Personal Memoirs of U. S. Grant,* ed. E. B. Long (Cleveland, OH, and New York: The World Publishing Company, 1952), 24.

41. Bauer, 46.

42. Eisenhower, 63–64.

43. Ibid., 64.

44. Ibid.

45. Ibid.

46. Ibid., 64–65; Bauer, 42, 46–48; Heidler and Heidler, 60–61; McAfee and Robinson, 137.

47. McAfee and Robinson, 137.

48. Heidler and Heidler, 61–63;

49. According to Richard Bruce Winders, "The U.S. Army had employed a type of artillery known as 'flying artillery,' which dramatically increased the mobility and fire of that arm of the service. Whereas on the past North American battlefields cannon were drawn onto the battlefield by hand or draught animals and were left in one place, the U.S. Artillery at Palo Alto performed differently. Each gun had its own horse-drawn limber that contained a supply of ammunition. In addition, each member of the gun crew had his own mount. Thus, the unit could gallop anywhere on the battlefield that it was needed, unhook its guns, and unleash a storm of shot, shell, or canister against its surprised foe." Winders, 97.

50. Ibid., 96–97; Heidler and Heidler, 61–63; Eisenhower, 76–85.

51. Heidler and Heidler, 65.

52. Paul C. Nagel, *John Quincy Adams, a Public Life, a Private Life* (New York: Alfred A. Knopf, 1998), 405.

53. Heidler and Heidler, 141–145.

54. T. R. Fehrenbach, *Fire and Blood: A History of Mexico* (New York: Da Capo Press, 1995), 401–402.

55. Heidler and Heidler, 145.

Chapter 2

The US Army and Mexican Border Security, 1850–61

The Texans having vainly endeavored to get government troops to afford them protection took the matter in their own hand, but their management has been so rash and ill judged as to have only served to aggravate the evil.

North American and United States Gazette,
8 November 1855

The whole frontier is laid waste.

Major S. P. Heintzelman's Official Report,
27 December 1859

I have been directed by the . . . Sec'y of War of the U.S. to notify the Mexican authorities on the Rio Grande, that they must break up and disperse the bands of banditti concerned in the outrages against the persons and property of American citizens.

Colonel Robert E. Lee, 12 April 1860

Border Geography

The new border with Mexico stretched more than 1,900 miles over rough and difficult terrain. Starting at the Gulf of Mexico near the towns of Brownsville and Matamoros, the border followed the Rio Grande for 1,254 miles to a point just north of El Paso, Texas.[1] While the lower Rio Grande was for the most part "plains country," the valley of the Rio Grande, which ran from the lower Rio Grande to El Paso, contained several irregular mountain ranges, including the Guadalupe Mountains of west Texas. "The Rio Grande is a storm-water stream, subject to great and sudden floods," noted the *Geographical Review*. "The valley floor of the basin has a growth of grasses and stunted shrubs. Along the river bottoms are cottonwood trees. On the slopes at the basin margin with the lower elevations are yucca and cactus and higher up there is a scrubby growth of juniper, cedar, and oak."[2] North of El Paso, the border turned westward running 533 miles to the Colorado River. This area was described as "lowlands with an extreme desert climate."[3] The southeastern region of Arizona also contained a large group of mountain ranges connected to the Sierra Madre of Mexico. From the lower Colorado River, the border extended north 24 miles and then due west 141 miles to San Diego, California. The entire 1,952-mile border was diverse but could generally be "characterized by deserts, rugged mountains, abundant sunshine and by two major rivers—the Colorado River and the

Rio Grande (Rio Bravo del Norte)—which provide life-giving waters to the largely arid but fertile lands along the rivers in both countries."[4] On both sides of the border, the population remained scattered and sparse.

Deployment of US Army Forces on the Mexican Border

With the close of the Mexican War, a large portion of the Regular Army returned to frontier protection duties. Reduced to less than 10,000 soldiers, the US Army faced innumerable challenges.[5] Even though the new border with Mexico stretched more than 1,900 miles, Congress had little or no sense of urgency to increase the size of the peacetime Army. To make matters worse, one provision of the Treaty of Guadalupe stipulated that the United States was responsible for thwarting Indian attacks from the United States into Mexico. Many of the Comanche raids aimed at Mexico came out of the north near the Red River, far removed from the border.[6]

In 1849, in an effort to protect Mexicans and Texans, the US Army established nine new forts. Running from Fort Worth in the north to Fort Duncan on the Rio Grande, the posts were designed to provide a modicum of protection to the civilian population. Unfortunately, the US Army lacked enough mounted troops to occupy the new fortifications. According to Colonel Harold B. Simpson, "These posts were well located and strategically placed and might have provided the protection needed had they been adequately garrisoned and manned by mounted rather than by foot soldiers."[7] Remarkably, many of these forts contained less than 50 infantrymen, leading one distraught Texan to ask his political representatives if they might "conceive of anything more absurd than starting in pursuit of flying Comanche in a wagon drawn by mules."[8]

From 1849 to 1851, the US Army was so shorthanded it was forced to call on the services of the legendary Texas Rangers. While the Rangers' fighting prowess was second to none, the US Army was often hesitant to request their services from the Governor of Texas. Although US Army Brevet Major General George M. Brooke federalized four companies of Rangers in 1849 for 2 years of service, he was aware of the possible pitfalls associated with their use. "Their feelings, and, you may say, general and natural hostility to Indians, would be very apt to bring about what we wish to avoid—a general war," he told his superiors.[9]

By the early 1850s, the US Army increased its mounted presence in Texas, adding five companies of mounted rifles and seven new forts. These new efforts helped the Army and Texas Rangers cut off many of the Indian trails leading into Mexico. However, as author James R. Arnold points out:

The Comanches responded in the same way the North Vietnamese would respond to American efforts to interdict passage along the Ho Chi Minh Trail in the 1960s; they made new trails, farther away from military bases. . . . The army in Texas discovered, as would their successors in Vietnam one hundred or so years in the future, that its ability to provide security for civilians did not extend beyond gunshot range of its outpost.[10]

Although the US Army positioned 2,300 soldiers in the Department of Texas, only 600 manned the forts along the Rio Grande. It soon became apparent they could not possibly stop all the attacks. (See map 3.) Therefore, in 1852, the United States scrapped the provision in the Treaty of Guadalupe Hidalgo, which required them to defend Mexico against Indian attacks.[11] According to historian Clarence C. Clendenen, the provision was removed "because of the complete impossibility of carrying it out."[12] He went on to point out, "In its efforts to cover the entire frontier in the early 1850s, the

Map 3. Major Comanche Trail Into Mexico.

army frequently resembled a man who is trying to be in two or three places at once."[13] According to historian Robert Wooster:

> Officials soon realized that the small regular establishment could not guard each settlement along the ever-changing frontier. In addition, the great distances between the largest bases meant that both Indians and whites could pass undetected by army patrols. Recognizing the failure of traditional defensive lines, a number of officers hoped to abandon the smaller posts and concentrate troops at important strategic points. From these central positions commanders could send regular patrols and expeditions into Indian lands. By showing the country's military might, it was believed, such columns would persuade the Indians to give up armed resistance.[14]

The new plan was doomed from the start. In most cases, soldiers sent to overawe and pursue the Indians found to their dismay their foe would simply vanish into the vast landscape or elude the Army by crossing the Rio Grande. As Wooster points out, "There were not enough troops to make a distinct impression, and even mounted regiments found that catching the fleet warriors of the southern plains was a tremendously difficult undertaking." Public outrage over Army plans to vacate its smaller forts created a political firestorm, forcing the Army to occupy almost all of its small posts.[15]

In 1853, Secretary of War Jefferson Davis dispatched Colonel Joseph K. Mansfield on an inspection tour of frontier forts. Mansfield identified a major gap in security along the Rio Grande, reporting that El Paso was defenseless and without a fort. He also noted that there was no fort between El Paso and Fort Clark. "Probably as a result of Mansfield's report and problems with the Apaches between El Paso and Fort Clark," wrote historians J. E. Kaufmann and H. W. Kaufmann, "the army filled the gap, adding Fort Bliss, Fort Stockton and Fort Davis." In yet another inspection of the Rio Grande posts, Mansfield found Fort McIntosh and Fort Brown lacking proper defenses and most of the soldiers stationed there living in tents.[16]

In 1854, a Texan living on the Rio Grande wrote a letter to the Governor of Texas complaining about the lack of security. "I do not know how you can help us. The nine companies of infantry here have not twenty horses in their stables. The rifles [mounted rifles] are sixty miles off, and before we can send news to them of depredations the Indians are gone beyond pursuit."[17] Clearly, the US Army's expanded fort system had little effect on border security. Infantry was of little use in chasing down mounted raiders, while US Army mounted forces were spread so thinly they, too, proved practically worthless.

By 1855, Congress increased the size of the US Army and stationed 3,449 soldiers in Texas. Of this number, only 1,364 were actually positioned along the border. One of the units sent to Texas included the newly raised 2d Cavalry Regiment. While additional cavalry troops were sorely needed, they were still not enough to fully secure the border. "It is obvious," wrote Clendenen, "that the 'high command' of the Department of Texas did not anticipate any serious trouble from the direction of Mexico. The danger that caused real concern was from the north and west. The troops were deployed facing in the direction from which trouble was anticipated."[18]

A list of forts along the Rio Grande from New Mexico to Texas included Conrad, Craig, Thorn, Fillmore, Bliss, Quitman, Davis, Clark, Duncan, McIntosh, Ringgold, and Brown. By all accounts, the posts were greatly undermanned. Assigned to these primitive, isolated forts, the soldiers continued to battle Indians and boredom, while the lingering hatred between the Mexicans and the Texans further complicated the US Army's mission along the border.[19]

Captain James H. Callahan and the Burning of Piedras Negras

An example of the Army's perplexing work in this area is underscored in an operation conducted by Captain James H. Callahan of the Texas Rangers. Using the doctrine of hot pursuit to cloak a slave-hunting expedition into Mexico, Callahan and his Rangers, accompanied by a party of American mercenaries, crossed the Rio Grande near Eagle Pass on 1 October 1855. Two days later, Callahan and his men encountered a sizable force of Mexican soldiers and their Indian allies. In the ensuing melee, approximately 18 individuals were killed or wounded. As the Mexicans and Indians withdrew, Callahan and his men seized control of the Mexican town of Piedras Negras. Convinced that a large Mexican military contingent was headed toward the town, Callahan urgently requested the assistance of US soldiers at nearby Fort Duncan to cover his river crossing. Captain Sidney Burbank responded by moving cannons into position to protect Callahan's crossing site. A rapid rise in the river, however, caused the Texans to postpone their passage, forcing Callahan to fortify Piedras Negras against a possible attack. On 6 October, as the Texans began crossing to the American side of the Rio Grande, the Mexican Army arrived outside the town. This time, Callahan's calls for US Army assistance were met with a "decided refusal" by Captain Burbank. Before crossing back into Texas, Callahan's men sacked and burned the Mexican town to the ground.[20] In his book *Lone Star Justice: The First Century of the Texas Rangers*, Robert M. Utley wrote:

> Viewed from any perspective, the Callahan expedition was a fiasco. Even the most liberal interpretation of the doctrine of hot pursuit could not justify what in fact was a filibustering expedition aimed principally at recovery of runaway slaves, carried out by a captain and sixty Rangers in the service of the state of Texas, joined by nearly as many buccaneers in the service of Texas cotton planters.[21]

While the Mexicans were rightfully outraged by the provocative actions of the Texans, Callahan's actions were praised by his fellow citizens. Outside of Texas, however, the American press remained highly skeptical of Callahan and his Texas Rangers. The *North American and United States Gazette* noted that Callahan "gathered his men, and after vainly endeavoring to find the Indians, took it for granted that they had retreated to the other side of the Rio Grande, and therefore marched thither to invade Mexico, in order to attack them. They have invaded Mexico without the requisite force and justification, burnt a Mexican town, fought a useless battle and barely made good their escape."[22] Were it not for Burbank's reassessment of the implications of US Army involvement in Callahan's scheme, the United States and Mexico might once again have been brought to the brink of war.

Over the next few years, the US Army continued its efforts to combat Indian raids throughout the region. The ongoing political instability in Mexico (a theme that would complicate border security efforts for decades) meant that the US Army could count on only limited support from the Mexican Army. By the late 1850s, Mexico was again engulfed in a bloody civil war. This time, the contest centered on the role of the church and pitted the conservatives (the church and the army) against the liberals. From 1858 to 1861, in what became known as the Reform War, the two sides battled for supremacy. In January 1861, the liberals finally shattered the conservatives and occupied Mexico City, electing Benito Juarez as the new President of Mexico.[23]

In 1858, while Mexican liberals and conservatives fought for supremacy, the US Army found itself stretched to the limit. With soldiers operating against the Mormons in Utah and attempting to maintain the peace in Kansas, the Army struggled with limited resources to protect the frontier. "The want of troops to give reasonable security to our citizens in distant settlements . . . can scarcely be too strongly stated," wrote

General in Chief Winfield Scott to the Secretary of War. "I will only add," he continued, "that as often as we have been obliged to withdraw troops from one frontier in order to reinforce another, the weakened points have been instantly attacked or threatened with formidable invasion."[24] On the Texas-Mexico border, Scott's observation proved prophetic.

Convinced that the Comanches and other Plains Indian tribes were poised to strike deep into Texas in early 1859, Brevet Major General David E. Twiggs, the new Department of Texas Commander, prepared to launch a preemptive strike. The 70-year-old Twiggs planned to pull his troops out of Forts Brown, Ringgold, and McIntosh and consolidate a cavalry strike force in the Indian territory. Although he intended to reinforce Fort Duncan, this bold move would leave the lower Rio Grande defenseless. "Outposts on the Rio Grande had always been expensive," wrote James Arnold. "Twiggs reckoned that rather than fetter his scarce manpower at near-useless posts, he would abandon garrisons along the Rio Grande."[25] Faced with limited resources, Winfield Scott approved Twiggs's plan. Although the Texans along the Rio Grande were outraged and voiced their disapproval to Washington, Twiggs evacuated the forts along the lower Rio Grande and moved his soldiers north.[26] Astoundingly, Twiggs's adjustments left only one cavalry company to patrol the vast territory between the Rio Grande and San Antonio.[27]

Cortina's War

By the summer of 1859, relations between Mexican-Americans and Anglos in border towns like Brownsville, Texas, were exceedingly strained. According to Utley, "Mexicans of every station on both sides of the border hated the gringos for the Mexican War and for the oppression that followed."[28] Clendenen, on the other hand, wrote that "many Americans, with their point of view warped by the memories and myths of the recent war and the Texas rebellion, were fully convinced that all Mexicans were treacherous, undependable and cruel."[29]

This volatile state of affairs ignited on 13 July 1859 when Juan Nepomuceno Cortina shot and wounded the Brownsville city marshal who had beaten one of Cortina's former employees. A well-known Mexican whose mother owned a large ranch north of Brownsville, Cortina had long resented the intolerance and injustice displayed by whites toward his Mexican brethren. After gunning down the marshal, Cortina fled to Matamoros. By the time he arrived in Mexico, his violent encounter with the Anglo establishment had transformed him into a champion of oppressed Mexicans. While many Mexicans lauded his actions, Cortina was considered by many Anglos to be nothing more than a trifling bandit.[30]

Cortina remained in seclusion for more than 2 months, but on 28 September, he raided Brownsville, murdering four men and liberating the Mexicans held in the local jail. After running roughshod over the terrified Anglo population for nearly 24 hours, prominent citizens in Matamoros, perhaps fearing American reprisals, persuaded Cortina to leave Brownsville. Late in the afternoon, Cortina, accompanied by approximately 80 men, headed north. To ensure the protection of American citizens in Brownsville, a Mexican militia force from Matamoros crossed the Rio Grande and occupied the vacant Fort Brown. It was a surprising turn of events indeed. A Mexican military force crossed over onto US soil and occupied a fort abandoned by the US Army to protect xenophobic American citizens from a vengeful Mexican insurgent.[31] A letter written at Point Isabel, Texas, and reprinted in *The Charleston Mercury* exposed perhaps the true nature of the events in Brownsville:

> The facts are simply these: There are a lot of bad characters who have been imposing upon, murdering, robbing and maltreating the Mexicans. It got to such a pass that the rancheros thought it high time to strike a blow in self-defence, and exterminate these American evil doers at one blow. . . . If there had been a garrison at Fort Brown the thing would not have happened, as the Mexicans have a great awe of the '*soldados*.' There is no doubt but that the Government has displayed a most wanton disregard for the interests of this frontier, in withdrawing every soldier for a line of over 400 or 500 miles in extent, on the borders of a country infested with thieves, murderers and wild Indians.[32]

The political fallout from Cortina's Brownsville raid was swift. With investors and politicians clamoring for protection, President James Buchanan directed the Secretary of War to order the US Army to return to the lower Rio Grande. General Twiggs, who was in San Antonio, promptly ordered two companies from Fort Clark back to Fort Brown. As the companies marched south to Fort Brown, Twiggs was bombarded with troublesome stories of a new massacre at Brownsville and the burning of the town by Cortina. Twiggs also received news that Cortina was marching on the Nueces River with an army of 800 men. Twiggs immediately ordered a company from the 2d Cavalry Regiment, four companies of infantry, and two artillery companies to the Nueces, under the command of Major Samuel P. Heintzelman. In Washington, the Secretary of War alerted US Army commands in Kansas and Louisiana of a possible movement to the lower Rio Grande. To his great embarrassment, Twiggs was informed that the latest intelligence regarding Cortina and the burning of Brownsville was false. While Washington halted the troop movements from Kansas and Louisiana, Twiggs ordered Heintzelman to continue on to Fort Brown. According to Clendenen, Twiggs ordered Major Heintzelman to "spare no effort to bring Cortina to battle and use every means at his disposal to destroy Cortina's band. Marauders would be pursued to the Rio Grande, but the United States troops would not cross the river unless in 'hot pursuit.'"[33]

The citizens of Brownsville were disappointed to hear that not all the soldiers were coming to their rescue. A correspondent in Brownsville reported:

> We in Brownsville have learned with much regret that the American government have countermanded the order given to troops that were ordered to Fort Brown. God knows what they mean. Are we to be considered as belonging to the United States, or are we not? It is really too scandalous. We have now been more than two months on guard, and are just as badly off as at the commencement of the disturbance; I may say, indeed, more so, for the bandit Cortinas [sic] is daily increasing his force, and the United States will find to their cost, that no 200 or 300 troops will put a stop to this invasion and mutiny, unless something is done promptly.[34]

Meanwhile in Brownsville, Cortina demanded the release of Tomas Cabrera, one of his officers who had been captured and locked in the town jail. When authorities refused his request, Cortina moved several hundred of his men across the Rio Grande, taking up a defensive position on his mother's ranch north of Brownsville. On 25 October, a small force of Brownsville volunteers, Mexican militia from Matamoros, and approximately 40 apathetic Mexican civilians marched on Cortina's position. The heterogeneous posse also brought along two small cannons. In the attack that followed, Cortina and his men quickly routed the confused rabble, driving them back into Brownsville and, in the process, captured both artillery pieces. One local newspaper reported the thrashing was so complete that it was too "painful for us to chronicle."[35] When Heintzelman learned of the battle, he filed a report noting that, not long after the first shots were fired, each man in the posse seemed "anxious to be the first to reach Brownsville."[36]

By the time Heintzelman arrived at Fort Brown on 5 December, the Texas Rangers who had been ordered to Brownsville by Texas Governor

Hardin R. Runnels had already ignited an even larger firestorm. On 13 November, the Rangers, under the command of Captain William G. Tobin, dragged Cabrera from the Brownsville jail and lynched him. The provocative action served to further infuriate Cortina and persuaded even more Mexicans to flock to his banner. Toward the end of November, the Rangers and volunteers from Brownsville attacked Cortina again. They, too, were quickly routed. As word spread rapidly that Cortina intended to drive the Americans out of Texas, more recruits rushed to join him.[37]

Heintzelman wasted little time in attacking Cortina. Early on the morning of 14 December, Heintzelman marched north out of Brownsville with his force of Regulars and Tobin's Texas Rangers. At sunup, Heintzelman found Cortina's ranch empty and ordered his men to continue moving north. After marching about 3 miles, Heintzelman discovered a small command of *Cortinistas*. With the US Army soldiers and artillery providing the backbone for Tobin's apprehensive Rangers, Heintzelman quickly overpowered the Mexicans, scattering them in all directions. Heintzelman was not impressed with Tobin and his men. "We would undoubtedly have done better without the Rangers," he concluded in his report. That night, however, Major John Salmon Ford's company of Texas Rangers arrived to reinforce Heintzelman. Ford and his Rangers far surpassed Tobin's men in discipline and fighting capabilities. A substantial rainstorm overnight ruined most of the gunpowder, causing Heintzelman and his command to abandon their pursuit of Cortina and return to Brownsville.[38]

Determined to either destroy Cortina or drive him out of Texas, Heintzelman and 150 soldiers, two companies of Rangers, and two large howitzers left Brownsville once again on 21 December. On 26 December, Ford's intrepid scouts informed Heintzelman that Cortina and most of his command were at Rio Grande City. Heintzelman also learned that some of Cortina's command was occupying the abandoned US Army post at Fort Ringgold. About 2200 that night, Cortina changed camp sites, pulling his men out of Rio Grande City and leaving only a few pickets around Fort Ringgold.[39] A little after midnight on 27 December, in an almost impenetrable fog, the soldiers and Rangers moved silently toward Rio Grande City. Ford's Ranger command was to infiltrate past the Mexican forward outposts and take up blocking positions in their rear while Tobin's Rangers assaulted Cortina's right flank. Heintzelman planned to attack Cortina's center 30 minutes after Tobin launched his attack.

Ford soon found that he could not work his way past the Mexican sentries without being detected. He, therefore, decided to charge directly into Cortina's camp. The Mexicans fired blindly into the fog with the two artillery pieces they had previously seized and managed to launch a small countercharge against Ford's Rangers. It was to no avail. Although more than a dozen of his men were wounded, Ford drove home his attack. While Cortina managed to save his guns, his men abandoned nearly all their equipment on the field as they fled north toward the town of Roma or into the river. By the time Heintzelman and Tobin reached the field, the fog had lifted, and Cortina's artillery could be seen moving rapidly north toward Roma. Heintzelman ordered Ford to pursue the guns. While Ford and his Rangers rode north, Heintzelman's cavalry killed a number of the *Cortinistas* running toward the Rio Grande. Once at the river, the US cavalry troops dismounted and, using their new Sharps carbines, shot and killed many of the Mexicans trying to swim the river.[40] "We had fourteen Rangers wounded," Heintzelman wrote in his official report. "We killed some sixty of his [Cortina's] men. Persons who counted his men in town yesterday say that he had with him over five hundred and fifty men. He retreated so rapidly that at no time was more than a small portion of the command engaged."[41] Cortina managed to escape the melee by swimming the Rio Grande. Although he continued his raids for another 20 years, the combined efforts of the US Army and Texas Rangers had at least forced him out of Texas.

In February 1860, Brevet Colonel Robert E. Lee temporarily replaced Twiggs as the Commander of the Department of Texas. Lee arrived in Texas with two letters from the Secretary of War, granting him wide discretion in his dealings with the Mexicans. One letter authorized Lee to go "beyond the limits of the United States" in pursuing Cortina. The other letter authorized him to attack the "banditti" in Mexico if the Mexican military authorities failed to break up Cortina's band. In March, Lee allowed about 200 soldiers and Rangers to cross into Mexico in search of Cortina. When the local military commander protested the incursion, Lee informed him that he "had been directed by the honorable Secretary of War . . . to notify the Mexican authorities that they must break up and disperse the bands of banditti concerned in the outrages. . . . I shall, therefore consider it my duty to hold them [the Mexican officials] responsible for its faithful performance."[42] Unfortunately, neither Lee nor the Mexican Government could do little to stop the continued raids across the border. According to James Arnold, "Lee concluded that Indians, Mexicans, and Americans would commit crimes when it could be done with impunity. He judged that it would require twenty thousand troops to defend adequately the region's isolated ranches and small towns."[43] In the end, Lee's small incursion into Mexico proved only a minor incident. Larger, more ominous tribulations were on the horizon.

Summary

From the end of the Mexican War until 1861, the US Army's ability to defend the US-Mexican border was hindered by a paucity of troops. The small detachments of infantry soldiers assigned to the primitive posts along the Rio Grande could not contend with the fast-moving Comanches or, for that matter, with mounted bandits and other criminal elements. Additional cavalry forces proved of limited value as the vastness of the territory limited their effectiveness. Furthermore, continuous political instability in Mexico limited joint efforts between the US Army and Mexican military forces.

Captain Callahan's raid into Mexico and the subsequent burning of Piedras Negras highlighted for the US Army the problems associated with containing overzealous law enforcement officers and adventurers. Throughout the course of US Army involvement on the Mexican border, these elements often provoked both the Mexican-American and Mexican populations, further fanning the flames of extremism. Cortina's war brought to light the profound hatred between Texans, Mexican-Americans, and Mexicans, and perceived injustice and intolerance gave impetus to Cortina's uprising. It is indeed ironic that, to quell Cortina's rebellion, the US Army was forced to call to its assistance organizations that at times had helped foster the outbreaks of violence.

During this period, the US Government and the US Army tried to maintain a harmonious relationship with Mexico. While both the State Department and the Army were certainly aware of the pitfalls of crossing into Mexican territory and violating international law, both entities were willing to sanction such action if the need arose. Interestingly, many of the major issues that confronted the US Army in the mid-19th century reappeared in the early 20th century.

Notes

1. "The International Boundary and Water Commission, Its Mission, Organization and Procedures for Solution of Boundary and Water Problems," *International Boundary and Water Commission*, 2, http://www.ibwc.state.gov/html/about_us.html

2. "The Frontier Region of Mexico: Notes to Accompany a Map of the Frontier," *Geographical Review*, Vol. 3, No. 1 (January 1917), 20–21.

3. Ibid., 20.

4. "The International Boundary and Water Commission," 2.

5. Clarence C. Clendenen, *Blood on the Border: The United States Army and the Mexican Irregulars* (London: The Macmillan Company, 1969), 7.

6. Colonel Harold B. Simpson, *Cry Comanche: The 2nd U.S. Cavalry in Texas, 1855–1861* (Hillsboro, TX: Hill Junior College Press, 1979), 54.

7. Ibid., 55.

8. James R. Arnold, *Jeff Davis's Own: Cavalry, Comanches, and the Battle for the Texas Frontier* (New York: John Wiley & Sons, Inc., 2000), 16.

9. Robert M. Utley, *Lone Star Justice: The First Century of the Texas Rangers* (New York: Oxford University Press, 2002), 87–93.

10. Arnold, 15–16.

11. Clendenen, 11.

12. Ibid.

13. Ibid., 8.

14. Robert Wooster, *Soldiers, Sutlers, and Settlers: Garrison Life on the Texas Frontier* (College Station: Texas A&M University Press, 1987), 141.

15. Ibid.

16. J. E. Kaufmann and H. W. Kaufmann, *Fortress America: The Forts That Defended America, 1600 to the Present* (Cambridge, MA: Da Capo Press, 2004), 200.

17. Arnold, 16.

18. Clendenen, 11.

19. Francis Paul Prucha, *A Guide to the Military Post of the United States, 1789–1895* (Madison: The State Historical Society of Wisconsin, 1964), 45–46.

20. Ibid, 19; Utley, 95–97.

21. Utley, 97.

22. *North American and United States Gazette* (Philadelphia), 8 November 1855.

23. Lynn V. Foster, *A Brief History of Mexico* (New York: Facts on File Inc., 1997), 130–131.

24. Clendenen, 12–13.

25. Arnold, 262.

26. Clendenen, 12–13.

27. Arnold, 263.

28. Utley, 109.

29. Clendenen, 18.

30. Utley, 109; Clendenen, 22.

31. Utley, 109; Clendenen, 22.

32. *The Charleston Mercury* (Charleston, SC), 7 October 1859.

33. Clendenen, 24–25.

34. *The New York Herald* (New York), 17 December 1859.

35. Utley, 110.

36. Clendenen, 27.

37. Utley, 111.

38. Clendenen, 30–31; Utley, 112.

39. "Official Report S. P. Heintzelman," *Daily National Intelligencer*, 25 January 1860.

40. Clendenen, 32–34; Utley, 113.

41. "Official Report S. P. Heintzelman."

42. Clendenen, 38–42.

43. Arnold, 279.

Chapter 3

The US Army and Mexican Border Security, 1865–1910

> If we got into a war and drove out the French, we could not get out ourselves.
>
> Secretary of State William Henry Seward

> A useful way to approach the military campaigns of the 1870s is to understand the United States and Mexican armies as the pivotal forces in a transformation of the Rio Grande from a 'frontier' into a 'border.'
>
> James N. Leiker,
> *Racial Borders: Black Soldiers Along the Rio Grande*

> I want you to control and hold down the situation, and to do it in your own way. . . . I want you to be bold, enterprising, and at all times full of energy, when you begin, let it be a campaign of annihilation, obliteration and complete destruction. . . . I think you understand what I want done, and the way you should employ your forces.
>
> Major General Philip H. Sheridan to
> Colonel Ranald Slidell Mackenzie, April 1873

Major General Sheridan and Napoleon III on the Rio Grande

Mexico's vicious Reform War had barely ended when the American Civil War erupted in 1861. Strapped for cash, Mexican President Benito Juarez imposed a 2-year moratorium on payment of his foreign debt. In 1862, as Union and Confederate forces battled for supremacy in the United States, French, British, and Spanish troops landed in Veracruz, Mexico, intent on forcing Juarez's liberal government to pay them the money they were owed. Not content to merely recoup his foreign loans, Napoleon III of France sought to expand his imperial domain and conspired to capture all of Mexico. Mexican conservatives and the church aligned themselves with the French against Juarez and his liberal government. Voicing their disapproval of France's intention, England and Spain removed their soldiers from Veracruz. With the other European powers gone and with the United States preoccupied with its own Civil War, French troops marched on Puebla, Mexico. They were soundly defeated by Mexican forces under the command of General Ignacio Zaragoza and Porfirio Diaz on 5 May (Cinco de Mayo). The French were forced to wait for reinforcements before continuing their conquest of Mexico.

When 30,000 additional French soldiers finally arrived, they quickly vanquished the liberal army, forcing Juarez and his government to flee to northern Mexico. In May 1864, Austrian Archduke Ferdinand Maximilian arrived in Mexico City. Conscripted with the help of Mexican conservatives to aid the church and their own crumbling influence, Maximilian was installed as Napoleon III's new puppet emperor.[1]

With the tentative end of the Civil War and the assassination of President Abraham Lincoln in April 1865, Secretary of State William H. Seward and the new President, Andrew Johnson, endeavored to maintain Lincoln's policy toward the French and Maximilian. Both men wanted the French and Maximilian out of Mexico but favored diplomatic means over force. "If we got into a war and drove out the French, we could not get out ourselves," Seward warned.[2] The British minister to the United States, Sir Frederick Bruce, wrote to his government that Secretary of War Edwin Stanton "considered the prospects of organizing the country under Maximilian hopeless, that France would get tired of the pecuniary sacrifice it entailed for no object and would give up the cause, and that it would be absurd to go to war for a matter which will terminate of itself."[3] In June, Seward sent the French Government a communication informing it there would be no change in the policy of the United States toward Maximilian's regime.

In Washington, however, General in Chief Ulysses S. Grant maintained a point of view far removed from those of the President, the Secretary of State, and the Secretary of War. Unlike Johnson, Seward, and Stanton, Grant was unwavering in his commitment to promptly return Juarez and his liberal government to power. He was also a strong proponent of a vigorous military response. In his book *Sheridan the Inevitable*, Richard O'Connor notes that "General Grant was determined to restore the Mexican republic, not only because of his resentment over Maximilian's aid to the Confederacy, but because his sympathies were entirely with the Juarez government."[4] One reason for Grant's empathy toward the Mexican liberals was his close friendship with Matias Romero, the official representative of the Juarez government in Washington. "I believe that we can count him now as one of the best friends of our country," Romero informed his foreign ministry.[5]

To help implement his aggressive strategy, Grant called on the colorful, hard-nosed fighter, Major General Philip H. Sheridan. One of the most popular Union commanders of the Civil War, Sheridan was closely attuned to Grant's stance against the imperialists in Mexico. Unlike Grant's friend, Major General William T. Sherman, who believed the Mexicans had "failed in self-government," Sheridan stood squarely with Grant.[6] As Jasper Ridley notes in his work *Maximilian and Juarez*, "Sheridan was as keen a liberal in politics as Grant and supported the same causes; he too was eager to help the Mexican liberals get rid of Maximilian and the French."[7]

On 17 May 1865, Grant ordered Sheridan south to command US Army forces west of the Mississippi. His first order of business was to compel the surrender of Confederate forces still operating in Texas and Louisiana. "I think the Rio Grande should be strongly held whether the forces in Texas surrender or not and that no time should be lost in getting them there," Grant wrote to Sheridan. "If war is to be made, they will be in the right place."[8] In his memoirs, Sheridan recalled his interview with Grant before departing to his new command:

> At this same interview he informed me that there was an additional motive in sending me to the new command, a motive not explained by the instructions themselves, and went on to say that, as a matter of fact, he looked upon the invasion of Mexico by Maximilian as a part of the rebellion itself, because of the encouragement that invasion had received from the Confederacy, and that our success in putting down secession would never be complete till the French and Austrian invaders were compelled to quit the territory of our sister republic. With regard to this matter, though, he said it would be necessary for me to act with great circumspection, since the Secretary of State, Mr. Seward, was much opposed to the use of our troops along the border in any active way that would be likely to involve us in war with European powers.[9]

By the time Sheridan arrived at his headquarters in New Orleans, Confederate forces in Texas and Louisiana had already surrendered. Concerned that former Confederates were attempting to cross into Mexico, Sheridan ordered George Armstrong Custer's cavalry division to Houston, Texas, and Wesley Merritt's cavalry division to San Antonio in an effort to "make a strong showing of forces in Texas."[10] In combination with Custer's and Merritt's movements, an infantry division was sent to Galveston and another to Brazos Santiago. The IV Corps was ordered to Victoria, Texas, and a large portion of XXV Corps moved directly to Brownsville. "The object being," Sheridan remarked, "to prevent, as far as possible, the escaping Confederates from joining Maximilian. I asked for an increase of force to send to Texas—in fact, to concentrate at available points in the State an army strong enough to move against the invaders of Mexico if occasion demanded."[11]

By the time Sheridan's forces assembled in Texas, Juarez's army was in shambles. One senior US Army officer reported, "The French practically dominated northern Mexico. Juarez's poverty-ridden troops could not withstand the well-trained, fully equipped French. . . . Moreover, they were poorly fed, half were without guns and ammunition and medical supplies, and their officers were often factious, selfish, and ambitious."[12]

While Seward was determined to maintain a measured diplomatic response to the French, Sheridan was just as resolute to push forward Grant's aggressive agenda. On 1 June, Sheridan arrived in Brownsville, determined, as he put it, "to impress the Imperialist, as much as possible, with the idea that we intended hostilities."[13] Without delay, Sheridan sent scouts and spies into northern Mexico and ordered his troops on the lower Rio Grande to brandish their warlike intentions. To further inflame imperialist angst, Sheridan demanded the return of Confederate munitions that ex-Confederates gave the Mexican imperialist commander at Matamoros. Not wanting to anger the Americans, the commander of Matamoros quickly complied with Sheridan's demands. "These demands," Sheridan recalled, "backed up as they were by such a formidable show of force, created much agitation and demoralization among the Imperial troops, and measures looking to the abandonment of northern Mexico were forthwith adopted by those in authority."[14] Alarmed by Sheridan's actions, the French minister in Washington requested that Seward bring him under control. Steadfastly maintaining his diplomatic course, Seward forced Sheridan to cease his incendiary measures.[15] Sheridan was appalled, writing that, "A golden opportunity was lost, for we had ample excuse for crossing the boundary, but Mr. Seward, being . . . unalterably opposed to any act likely to involve us in war, insisted on his course of negotiation with Napoleon.[16]

For several months, Sheridan's forces maintained a nonthreatening posture along the border. During this time, Juarez's liberal army continued to be battered by the imperialist and, according to Sheridan, "almost succumbed."[17] In Washington, Grant continued to pressure Johnson, notifying the President that "he would have no hesitation in recommending that notice be given the French that foreign troops be withdrawn from this Continent and the people left free to govern themselves in their own way."[18] Seward, nonetheless, remained faithful to his diplomatic course.

Annoyed by the slow pace of Seward's diplomatic initiatives, Sheridan once again placed his Army in an aggressive stance. Toward the end of September 1865, the general went to San Antonio where he reviewed the

IV Corps and Merritt's cavalry division. Knowing his movements and pronouncements would make their way back to the French and Maximilian, the general announced that the soldiers at San Antonio were preparing for a campaign to drive the French out of Mexico. After stirring up a hornet's nest at San Antonio, Sheridan and a regiment of cavalry moved rapidly to Fort Duncan. "Here I opened communications with President Juarez," Sheridan recalled, "taking care not to do this in the dark. The greatest significance was ascribed to my action, it being reported most positively and with many specific details that I was only awaiting the arrival of the troops . . . to cross the Rio Grande in behalf of the Liberal cause."[19] To compound the growing French nervousness, Sheridan ordered a pontoon train to Brownsville.[20]

By October 1865, Sheridan's provocative maneuvers on the Rio Grande had produced the desired effects. "These reports and demonstrations," Sheridan stated, "resulted in alarming the Imperialist so much that they withdrew the French and Austrian soldiers from Matamoras, and practically abandoned the whole of northern Mexico as far down as Monterey, with the exception of Matamoras where General [Tomas] Mejia continued to hold on with a garrison of renegade Mexicans."[21] With the withdrawal of most of the French and Austrian soldiers from northern Mexico, Sheridan began leaving large quantities of "condemned" small arms, ammunition, and other military supplies at various points along the American side of the Rio Grande. These supplies soon fell into the hands of Juarez's liberal army. Undoubtedly, Sheridan's actions revived the liberal forces in northern Mexico and, according to Sheridan, allowed them "to place the affairs of the Republic on a substantial basis."[22]

In the end, Seward's protracted diplomatic efforts, combined with Sheridan's belligerent pomposity, produced the desired effect. As early as October 1865, Napoleon III recognized he had placed his army into a quagmire. Loath to go to war with the United States and facing growing problems with Prussia, he desperately sought an honorable means to remove his soldiers from Mexico.[23] Although the French Army would not evacuate Mexico until March 1867, many historians maintain Sheridan's efforts caused the French to leave well ahead of schedule.[24] Richard O'Connor points out that "historians have generally credited Sheridan with a skillful show of bluff and deception along the Mexican border which preserved the Monroe Doctrine's integrity and warned other intruders from the shores of the Western Hemisphere for many years."[25]

Following his capture by Juarez's army, Maximilian was shot to death by a firing squad on 19 June 1867. The execution of Maximilian and the destruction of the conservative forces ushered in a relatively stable period in Mexican history with the restoration of President Juarez and the Mexican Republic. Seward, Grant, and Sheridan contributed significantly to the liberal victory in Mexico. "Among the benefits of intervention," wrote Ralph Roeder, "not the least were the new ties with the United States, which broke the bonds of the past and coupled the two countries in common interest."[26] Indeed, American diplomatic support for Juarez, combined with the zealous actions of the US Army on the border, helped restore some goodwill between the two nations, an element previously torn asunder by the Mexican War.

President Benito Juarez ruled Mexico from 1867 to 1872. During this time, the country experienced a rekindling of democracy and made sizable steps toward modernization. "Until Juarez took control," one writer claims, "Mexico never was governed." Following his death in 1872, President Sebastian Lerdo de Tejada continued to promote Juarez's liberal agenda.[27] Lerdo, however, refused to construct railroads into northern Mexico and was vehemently opposed to linking Mexican railroads with those in the United States. "Let there be a desert between strength and weakness," he declared. According to historian T. R. Fehrenbach, Lerdo "feared connecting rail lines might someday serve the *norteamericanos* for a military invasion."[28]

Deployment of Army Forces on the Mexican Border, 1870–86

With the French departure and the execution of Maximilian, a portion of the Regular Army returned to guarding the Mexican border. By the early 1870s, 800 US Army troops occupied five forts along the border of Arizona and New Mexico, while an additional 2,500 soldiers manned eight posts on the Rio Grande. The forts on the Rio Grande were spaced roughly 100 miles apart, leaving sufficient room for marauders to conduct attacks on both sides of the border. (See map 4.) Running from south to north, they included Forts Brown, Ringgold, McIntosh, Duncan, Clark, Stockton, Quitman, and Bliss. According to historian James N. Leiker, "Sherman did try to maintain an equal ratio of infantry and cavalry, but the border's fourteen-hundred mile expanse necessitated a greater proportion of the latter." As in the 1850s, infantry forces assigned to guard the border were of limited worth. For many years, black soldiers, or Buffalo Soldiers as they were called, made up the majority of US Army units guarding the Rio Grande.[29] Historian Loyd M. Uglow describes the basic defensive measures the US Army used on the frontier:

> Major forts in Texas from 1868 to 1886 usually had garrisons ranging from two to five companies—approximately 100 to 300 men. One company normally manned a regular

Map 4. Forts in Texas.

subpost, and a detachment of two to fifteen men held a picket station in most cases.

As time passed, military authorities refined and improved tactics and doctrine for their units on patrol. In 1871, Colonel J. J. Reynolds, commanding the Department of Texas, kept half the strength of each major fort on patrols and scouts in the field. In his opinion such a policy extended 'the greatest protection possible to the frontier counties with the force at hand.'[30]

As in the past, the US Army's mission on the border proved both dangerous and confusing. "A useful way to approach the military campaigns of the 1870s," wrote Leiker, "is to understand the United States and Mexican armies as the pivotal forces in a transformation of the Rio Grande from a 'frontier' into a 'border.'"[31] The most important task facing the US Army during this period was stopping Indian raids from both sides of the border. "The incursions of Indians from one nation into the other," wrote Robert M. Utley, "disturbed relations between the United States and Mexico for years and, in the 1870s and 1880s, presented the U.S. Army with one of its severest challenges." The Army's efforts were hampered by a lack of soldiers, vast and intimidating terrain, and continued political upheaval in Mexico. From the late 1860s to the early 1870s the Buffalo Soldiers of the 9th Cavalry Regiment (for years, the only cavalry unit permanently assigned to guard the Rio Grande) tried valiantly to stop the raids of Indians and Mexican brigands across the Rio Grande. However, "it was too much for one regiment," wrote historian William H. Leckie. "The Ninth was spread too thin, their enemies were far too numerous, the region simply too vast, and the international boundary too porous for effective defense."[32] While US Army units constantly patrolled the region in search of trails and pillagers, they were unsuccessful for the most part in locating the enemy. When Indians attacked civilians on the frontier, news of the forays often took so long to reach the Army that hunting down the culprits proved impossible.[33] The result, as Utley points out, was that "U.S. units but rarely apprehended raiding parties from either side of the boundary. Fewer in numbers and often preoccupied with revolutionary concerns, Mexican troops achieved even less success."[34]

National loyalty and changing geography along the Rio Grande added to the US Army's plight. Sheridan maintained that many Mexican-Americans living in Texas clung to the belief that they were Mexican citizens, a claim complicated by the changing course of the Rio Grande. Sheridan reported that, occasionally, when the river changed course, it would "leave a slice of Mexico on our side of the river, and in some cases with inhabitants. . . . With an international line in such a muddle, I can read-ily see how hard it will be for officers to perform a duty so delicate."[35]

The US Army continued to police the border during the tenures of Juarez and Lerdo. Countering raids across the Rio Grande by bandits and hostile Indians became commonplace events for the US Army. In Mexico, President Lerdo could do little to stop the attacks, and therefore, accord-ing to Fehrenbach, he simply "pretended" there was no problem.[36] It is not surprising then that, on many occasions, the US Army brazenly launched its own raids into Mexico.

Colonel Ranald S. Mackenzie's Raid

Between 1873 and 1882, US Army contingents crossed the Mexican border more than 23 times. "These incursions," Fehrenbach suggests, "made a much deeper impression on the Mexican mind than on the North

American. Every Mexican schoolboy could recite them; most United States citizens never heard of them."[37] One notable example is Colonel Ranald S. Mackenzie's foray against the Kickapoo Indians in May 1873.

Between the late 1860s and early 1870s, numerous Indian tribes conducted raids across the border. By 1873, the Kickapoos posed the greatest threat along the Rio Grande. Invited by the Mexican Government to relocate from Kansas to northeast Mexico and thereby serve as a buffer against Kiowa and Comanche attacks, emigrating Kickapoos were brutally assaulted by Texans as they made their way to Mexico. Once firmly established on their new land, the Kickapoos struck back. For the unprovoked attacks on their emigrant parties, the tribe swore revenge on Texans, and deadly attacks on Texas border ranches became commonplace. Much of the plunder from these raids was sold in Mexico with the tacit approval of Mexican officials. Again, US Army border defenses could do little to stop them.[38]

Under political pressure to remedy the situation, President Grant ordered Colonel Ranald S. Mackenzie and his 4th Cavalry Regiment to the Rio Grande. An aggressive combat veteran, Mackenzie had been highly successful in operations against the Comanches. By April 1873, Mackenzie and his regiment were assembled at Fort Clark prepared to conduct operations against the Kickapoos. The importance of the mission was underscored by the presence of Secretary of War William W. Belknap and General Sheridan at the fort.[39]

For years, the Grant Administration had sought approval from the Mexican Government to cross into Mexico to deal with the Indian raiders. This request, however, fell of deaf ears as any Mexican President who asked his Congress to authorize the US Army to cross into Mexican territory faced severe political repercussions. A majority of Mexicans believed any intrusion by the US Army into Mexico not only would be violating their national sovereignty but would be humiliating as well. Not surprisingly, President Lerdo refused to ask the Mexican Congress to authorize any US military border crossings.[40]

At Fort Clark, Sheridan refused to be thwarted by Mexican politicians. "I want you to control and hold down the situation, and to do it in your own way," he told Mackenzie. "I want you to be bold, enterprising, and at all times full of energy, when you begin, let it be a campaign of annihilation, obliteration and complete destruction. . . . I think you understand what I want done, and the way you should employ your force." When Mackenzie asked for clarification regarding crossing the border, Sheridan responded instantly, telling Mackenzie, "Damn the orders! Damn the authority. You are to go ahead on your own plan of action, and your authority and backing shall be Gen. Grant and myself. With us behind you in whatever you do to clean up this situation, you can rest assured of the fullest support. You must assume the risk. We will assume the final responsibility should any result."[41]

Mackenzie wasted little time. He sent his scouts across the Rio Grande to locate the Kickapoo village while he placed his regiment under a strict training program. On 16 May, the scouts reported the location of the Kickapoo village. They had also located two other villages occupied by Lipan and Mescalero Indians. Situated 40 miles west of Piedras Negras, each village contained approximately 60 lodges. Although the scouts reported no warriors in the Kickapoo encampment, Mackenzie nonetheless crossed the border the next night with 400 soldiers of the 4th Cavalry Regiment. According to historian Michael D. Pierce, Mackenzie had learned during earlier Indian campaigns that "destroying lodges and supplies and taking hostages was as effective a blow to the Indians as killing warriors."[42]

Near the Mexican town of Remolino on the San Rodrigo River, Mackenzie's command struck the Kickapoo village on the morning of 18 May. Encountering nothing more than women, children, and the elderly, his soldiers burned the village to the ground, killing approximately 19 and capturing 40. Hearing gunfire nearby, the occupants of the Lipan and Mescalero villages fled. Taking full advantage of the situation, Mackenzie burned both encampments. The soldiers hastily collected their prisoners and the Indian horses and headed back toward the Rio Grande. Pierce notes that "as they rode through a nearby Mexican village, the cavalrymen were met with looks of hatred and threatening mutterings not calculated to increase their confidence. It was obvious that word of the American presence was by now widespread, and interception by regular Mexican soldiers or an aroused citizenry seemed likely."[43] Remarkably, after 60 hours in the saddle, the 4th Cavalry Regiment crossed the Rio Grande again without incident and returned to its posts on 19 May, having lost only one soldier killed and two wounded.

While the American press praised Mackenzie's actions, the majority of Mexicans condemned the raid, claiming it was nothing less than an American "invasion." Although the Mexican press and citizenry were outraged, the Mexican Government remained, for the most part, noncommittal.[44] Mackenzie's raid proved highly successful. Utley points out, "Three months after Remolino, 317 [Kickapoos] began the trek to the Indian Territory and two years later another 115 made the journey. Also, fearful of further punishment, those who remained in Mexico dramatically scaled down their Texas raids."[45]

By the mid-1870s, a combination of patrolling and swift offensive action into enemy sanctuaries was proving highly successful. As Uglow points out, "A static defense was of little value except in warding off attacks on remote mail and stage stations. Mounted patrols, coupled later with large-scale offensive operations against enemy sanctuaries, became the primary tactic of the Texas frontier army."[46] Mackenzie's raid clearly demonstrated that attacking the enemy in his sanctuary was far more effective than mere patrolling and maintaining a fixed defense. Nevertheless, success came at a price. Each new border crossing chipped away at the goodwill previously established between the United States and Mexico.

Brigadier General Edward Ord, William R. "Pecos Bill" Shafter, and Porfirio Diaz

After Mackenzie's successful raid against the Kickapoos, the border remained relatively quiet for several years. In 1876, however, the Lipans, Mescaleros, Apaches, and the remaining Kickapoos shattered the tranquility. The tribes left their villages in Mexico, crossed the Rio Grande, and launched new raids into Texas, leaving behind a path of death and destruction. Once again, adding to the mayhem was the old raider Juan Cortina, whose banditti rustled cattle and horses along the border. The tumult was further compounded as a revolution again engulfed Mexico, pitting President Sebastian Lerdo against General Porfirio Diaz, one of the heroes of Cinco de Mayo. Clearly, this new internal strife greatly limited the Mexican Army's ability to control its side of the border.[47]

To combat the growing violence, the new Commander of the Department of Texas, Brigadier General Edward O. C. Ord, called on one of his most trusted officers, Lieutenant Colonel William R. "Pecos Bill" Shafter. Shafter and the black soldiers of his 24th Infantry Regiment had gained a well-earned reputation as aggressive Indian fighters. Knowing full well that simple patrolling and static defense could do little to combat the constant incursions, Ord ordered Shafter to prepare for offensive operations inside Mexico. "Ord and Shafter," Utley wrote, "shared the belief that the best way of dealing with the new wave of marauding was to root out the marauders in their homes, as Mackenzie had done, even though it violated the territory of a friendly neighbor."[48]

Under orders from Ord to "scout into Mexico when ever [sic] you can follow a trail successfully," Shafter's command struck numerous Indian villages during the summer of 1876. Ord informed Shafter he was "perfectly sure that the President will make 'no ado' over our crossing. . . ."

While Grant had little to say on the subject, Ord faced a blistering attack from Congress over Shafter's cross-border raids. Even more disconcerting, the Mexican Government voiced disapproval for each raid conducted by Shafter, raising tensions between the two nations to a boiling point. At the same time, Ord was criticized by the Governor of Texas for not protecting American citizens along the border. With his military career on the line, Ord ordered Shafter to temporarily curtail his raids into Mexico for the time being.[49]

In 1877, General Diaz ousted President Lerdo. Diaz's incumbency set in motion a lengthy period of stability and modernization coupled with a heavy-handed dictatorship. Diaz had used the US Army cross-border raids into Mexico as a means to topple Lerdo. According to Utley, "Diaz had triumphed, in part by exploiting Mexican hostility toward the United States." Knowing full well that the survival of his new regime depended on broad support from the Mexican people, Diaz made it clear to Washington that he would no longer tolerate US Army raids into Mexico.[50]

Diaz's edicts, however, made little impact on Ord and Shafter. When two of Shafter's Mexican scouts were jailed in Piedras Negras in April 1877 for helping the Americans, Pecos Bill sent five companies into the Mexican town to free them. While there was no confrontation with the Mexican Army, Diaz complained bitterly to Washington. Further undermining Diaz was President Rutherford B. Hayes's order issued in June, authorizing the US Army to conduct hot pursuits into Mexico. "A sort of war of nerves developed between the new Mexican President and the new U.S. President," wrote Utley. "Hayes used Diaz's need for U.S. recognition as a lever to force Mexico to remedy the border situation, and Diaz used the U.S. demand for such a remedy, particularly for a treaty permitting border crossings in hot pursuit, as a lever to pry loose recognition."[51]

In September, Shafter conducted yet another cross-border raid into Mexico, further ratcheting up the tension between Mexico and the United States. In so doing, he barely avoided a battle with the Mexican Army. So heated was the controversy that Congress announced plans to hold hearings to investigate problems along the border. When Shafter was called before Congress to testify in January 1878, several members accused him of trying to start a war with Mexico. When asked for his thoughts on the situation, Pecos Bill responded to the committee that "in his opinion, the best solution to the border trouble was to demand that Mexico stop the raids and, if she failed, to declare war."[52]

President Hayes offered recognition to the Diaz government in the spring of 1878. However, the Mexican President still refused to cooperate in policing the border until Hays expunged his order of hot pursuit. With negotiations at an impasse, Mackenzie and Shafter brought the situation to a head in June 1878 when they crossed the border and openly confronted the Mexican Army. With more than 1,000 men, the two commanders challenged the Mexican Army to stop their encroachment on Mexican soil. While its army tried twice to block the Americans, the Mexicans had no stomach for a fight and fled before contact could be made. Having embarrassed the Mexicans, the US Army returned to its side of the river.[53]

Once again, the Mexicans were outraged. Diaz was mortified and discomfited by the continual American border crossings. Fearing further damage to his political standing, Diaz was forced to act. The Mexican President sent one of his best generals to the border and ordered his army to take aggressive action against raiders and criminal elements in Mexico. By the close of 1878, raids from Mexico into the United States had been greatly reduced. Undoubtedly, the US Army's cross-border raids into Mexico and increased enforcement by the Mexican Army contributed greatly to the reduction in attacks. However, it was the Army's continual forays into Mexico that caused Diaz to finally act. Utley points out that many US Army commanders were convinced that the Mexican Army's aggressive response to policing its side of the border was "motivated largely by humiliation at the repeated border crossings by U.S. troops."[54]

With the Mexican Government now fully committed to policing its side of the border, President Hays repealed his order of hot pursuit in early 1880. Under a new treaty with Diaz, both countries would have limited correlative rights to conduct hot pursuits across the border. By the summer of 1880, relations between the United States and Mexico had greatly improved. As an example, the US Army and the Mexican Army worked together in a limited fashion to hunt down Apaches under Victorio and Geronimo in the 1880s. By the end of the 1880s, the US Army and the Mexican Army, as Leiker earlier suggested, had indeed transformed the frontier into a border.[55]

Summary

During this period, US Army actions along the Mexican border were instrumental in driving the French out of Mexico, eliminating cross-border Indian raids, and forcing the Mexican Government to take responsibility for policing its side of the border. Sheridan's bold movements with the large forces at his disposal at the end of the Civil War caused the French Army to evacuate northern Mexico and prompted Napoleon III to accelerate his timetable for a complete withdrawal. Sheridan's actions also helped, albeit briefly, to reestablished a more harmonious relationship between the United States and Mexico.

When the greatly reduced peacetime Army returned to guarding the Mexican border in the mid-1860s, it was confronted with the same problems the US Army had experienced in the 1850s. Once again, infantry soldiers in fixed defensive positions could not stop raiders from crossing the border. Mounted patrols also proved of limited value due to the limited quantity of horse soldiers and the expansive nature of the terrain.

By the 1870s, the US Army's senior leaders were convinced that they could not stop raiders from crossing the border using only static defense and mounted patrols. One alternative to disrupting the raids was to conduct preemptive strikes on the raiders' Mexican sanctuaries. The other option was to convince the Mexican Government to police its side of the border. In the end, it was the cross-border offensive actions of Mackenzie and Shafter that greatly curtailed the Indian raids, thereby forcing Diaz and the Mexican Army to maintain order on their side of the border.

Notes

1. Lynn V. Foster, *A Brief History of Mexico* (New York: Facts on File, Inc., 1997), 131–133. See also Jasper Ridley, *Maximilian and Juarez* (New York: Ticknor & Fields, 1992); Michele Cunningham, *Mexico and Foreign Policy of Napoleon III* (Gordonsville, VA: Palgrave Macmillan, 2000); Count Egon Caesar Corti, *Maximilian and Charlotte of Mexico*, trans. Catherine Alison Phillips (New York: Alfred A. Knopf, 1928); Ernst Pitner, *Maximilian's Lieutenant: A Personal History of the Mexican Campaign, 1864-7*, trans. and ed. Gordon Etherington-Smith (Albuquerque: University of New Mexico Press, 1993); Halford L. Hoskins, "French Views of the Monroe Doctrine and the Mexican Expedition," *The Hispanic American Historical Review*, Vol. 4, No. 4 (November 1921); Frederic Bancroft, "The French in Mexico and the Monroe Doctrine," *Political Science Quarterly*, Vol. 11, No. 1 (March 1896).

2. Dean B. Mahin, *One War at a Time: The International Dimensions of the American Civil War* (Washington, DC: Brassey's, 1999), 272.

3. Ibid.

4. Ridley, 206; Richard O'Connor, *Sheridan the Inevitable* (Indianapolis, IN: The Bobbs-Merrill Company, Inc., 1953), 278.

5. Robert Ryal Miller, "Matias Romero: Mexican Minister to the United States During the Juarez-Maximilian Era," *The Hispanic American Historical Review*, Vol. 45, No. 2 (May 1965), 243.

6. In a letter to Major General H. W. Halleck, dated 17 September 1863, Sherman stated: "I do not see that his [Napoleon III] taking military possession of Mexico concerns us. We have as much territory now as we want. The Mexicans have failed in self-government, and it was a question as to what nation she should fall a prey. That is now solved, and I don't see that we are damaged." William Tecumseh Sherman, *Memoirs of General W. T. Sherman* (New York: The Library of America, 1990), 367.

7. Ridley, 222.

8. John Y. Simon, ed., *The Papers of Ulysses S. Grant, Volume 15: May–December 31, 1865* (Carbondale: Southern Illinois University Press, 1988), 44.

9. Philip H. Sheridan, *Personal Memoirs of P. H. Sheridan*, Vol. 2 (North Scituate, MA: Digital Scanning, Inc., 1999), 210.

10. Ibid., 211.

11. Ibid, 213.

12. Carl Coke Rister, *Border Command: General Phil Sheridan in the West* (Norman: University of Oklahoma Press, 1944), 15.

13. Sheridan, 214.

14. Ibid.

15. Rister, 17.

16. Sheridan, 214–215.

17. Ibid., 215.

18. Simon, 317.

19. Sheridan, 215.

20. Rister, 18; O'Connor, 281.

21. Sheridan, 216.

22. Ibid., 216–217; Rister, 18–19.

23. Mahin, 274–275.

24. David Baguley, *Napoleon III and His Regime: An Extravaganza* (Baton Rouge: Louisiana State University Press, 2000), 179; O'Connor, 286.

25. O'Connor, 286.

26. Ralph Roeder, *Juarez and His Mexico* (New York: The Viking Press, 1947), 662.

27. Foster, 134–135.

28. T. R. Fehrenbach, *Fire and Blood: A History of Mexico* (New York: Da Capo Press, 1995), 451.

29. James N. Leiker, *Racial Borders: Black Soldiers Along the Rio Grande* (College Station: Texas A&M University Press, 2002), 46; Robert M. Utley, *Frontier Regulars: The United States Army and the Indian, 1866–1890* (New York: Macmillan Publishing Co., Inc., 1973), 345.

30. Loyd M. Uglow, *Standing in the Gap: Army Outpost, Picket Stations, and the Pacification of the Texas Frontier, 1866–1886* (Fort Worth: Texas Christian University Press, 2002), 18.

31. Leiker, 45.

32. William H. Leckie, with Shirley A. Leckie, *The Buffalo Soldiers: A Narrative of the Black Cavalry in the West* (Revised Edition) (Norman: University of Oklahoma Press, 2003), 89.

33. Ibid., 87.

34. Utley, 344–345.

35. Leiker, 45.

36. Fehrenbach, 451.

37. Ibid., 453.

38. Utley, 345–346; Michael D. Pierce, *The Most Promising Young Officer: A Life of Ranald Slidell Mackenzie* (Norman: University of Oklahoma Press, 1993), 121–122.

39. Utley, 346; Pierce, 121.

40. Utley, 346.

41. Pierce, 124.

42. Utley, 346–347; Pierce, 126.

43. Utley, 346–347; Pierce, 131.

44. Pierce, 134–136.

45. Utley, 349.

46. Uglow, 4.

47. Utley, 349–350; Paul H. Carlson, *"Pecos Bill:" A Military Biography of William R. Shafter* (College Station: Texas A&M University Press, 1989), 88–89.

48. Utley, 350; Carlson, 89.

49. Carlson, 95.

50. Utley, 351.

51. Carlson, 99; Utley, 351–352.

52. Carlson, 104–105.

53. Utley, 354.

54. Ibid., 354–355.

55. Clarence C. Clendenen, *Blood on the Border: The United States Army and Mexican Irregulars* (London: The Macmillan Company, 1969), 100; Utley, 355; Leiker, 45.

Chapter 4

The US Army and Mexican Border Security, 1911–17

> On one side of the river the slogan was 'Kill the Gringos';
> on the other it was 'Kill the Greasers.'
>
> Walter Prescott Webb

> It is almost too much to hope that our own border can be
> protected by American troops.
>
> *The Washington Post*, 15 April 1915

> Secretary of War has designated you to command
> expedition into Mexico to capture Villa and his bandits.
>
> Colonel Omar Bundy to
> Brigadier General John J. Pershing, 11 March 1916

Diaz

General Porfirio Diaz ruled Mexico either directly or indirectly with an iron fist from 1876 to 1910. One writer insinuates that Diaz's maxim was, "Bread and the Club: bread for the army, bread for the bureaucrats, bread for the foreigners, and even bread for the church—and the club for the common people of Mexico and those who differed with him."[1] Convinced from the beginning that American industrialists would use force if necessary to gain access to railroad and mining interests in Mexico, Diaz felt compelled to promote massive American investment in his country. Knowing full well that the brutal regime would ensure some semblance of stability, North American investors flocked to Mexico. By the early 1900s, nearly 85 percent of mining operations in Mexico were American owned.[2]

Although Mexico made great strides under Diaz, there existed among many Mexicans a simmering animosity toward him and the United States. In truth, most of Diaz's accomplishments were constructed on the backs of the poor. As Robert E. Quirk points out in his book *The Mexican Revolution, 1914–1915*, "The façade of prosperity was a cruel illusion. . . . Most outsiders remained blissfully unaware of the extreme disparity between the wealthy few and the masses of the poor."[3]

Scores of Mexican-Americans and Mexicans on the border also harbored a seething bitterness toward Anglo-Americans. Although Mexicans and Mexican-Americans far outnumbered whites in the border regions, the Anglos firmly controlled the levers of power, both politically and economically. Bigotry and intolerance also played a major role in the antagonism between the Anglos and Mexicans. "Mexican-Anglo relations in the nineteenth century," wrote David Montejano, "were inconsistent and contradictory, but pointed to the formation of a 'race situation' a situation where ethnic or national prejudice provided a basis for separation and control. . . . In the late nineteenth century, these race sentiments, which drew heavily from the legacy of the Alamo and the Mexican War, were maintained and sharpened by market competition and property disputes.[4] In the 1880s, a keen English observer living temporarily in Texas noted "that it was difficult to convince Texans that Mexicans were human. The Mexican 'seems to be the Texan's natural enemy; he is treated like a dog, or perhaps, not so well'"[5] By the early 20th century, many Mexican-Americans had been forced off their land. In his book *The Militarization of the U.S.-Mexico Border, 1978–1992*, Timothy J. Dunn observed:

> By 1900 . . . through legal and illegal coercive means, these Texas-Mexican families had been largely dispossessed of their land, except a few border enclaves. They were replaced by Anglo elites such as the King family, whose enormous ranch covered more than 500,000 acres. Texas law enforcement authorities' participation in extralegal, coercive acquisitions of Texas-Mexican land by Anglo ranchers was so notorious that among mexicanos in the Lower Rio Grande Valley 'the Texas Rangers were known as 'los rinches de la Kinena'—the King Ranch Rangers— to underscore the belief that they acted as King's strong-arm agents."[6]

Huerta, Carranza, Villa, and Zapata

In 1910, Diaz broke his promise to step down as President and, instead, rigged his own reelection. Scores of Mexicans were incredulous when Diaz announced to the world he had garnered an astonishing 99 percent of the vote. As T. R. Fehrenbach explains, "This did more than merely make the Mexican regime ridiculous in the eyes of the world, it destroyed the last hope of many Mexicans for peaceful change."[7] Indeed, within months, Mexico was plunged into revolution.

Francisco Madero rose out of the ensuing chaos to be elected President of Mexico in 1911. In 1913, Madero was murdered by forces loyal to General Victoriano Huerta. Huerta quickly installed himself as Mexico's new strongman but was openly challenged by the forces of Venustiano Carranza, Francisco "Pancho" Villa, and Emiliano Zapata.

As violence in Mexico increased, President Howard Taft heightened the US Army troop presence along the border. In March 1911, Taft placed

30,000 soldiers on the border. However, as Clarence C. Clendenen points out, "most Americans were not deeply interested in Mexico and regarded the turmoil in that country as more a gaudy spectacle than anything else." Many Americans were, therefore, surprised by Taft's actions. In the end though, the troop movement proved somewhat anticlimactic and the majority of the soldiers were withdrawn in August, never having fired a shot.[8]

Deployment of US Army Forces on the Mexican Border

Although Huerta guaranteed Taft "peace and prosperity" in Mexico, by 1913 the country was fully engulfed in violence as Carranza and his followers battled the Mexican President for control. Shocked by Huerta's past behavior, Taft's replacement, President Woodrow Wilson, ordered the US Army's 2d Division to Texas, ended the arms embargo to anti-Huerta forces, and steadfastly refused to recognize the Huerta government.[9] The Army once again found its mission complicated by racial hatred between Anglos and Mexicans, the sheer size of the border, and a shortage of soldiers. According to historian Allan R. Millett:

> The responsibility of keeping the revolution south of the Rio Grande belonged in part to the United States Army. The army's main task was to prevent the organized battles for the Mexican border towns from including the neighboring American towns. Since American troops were ordered not to cross the border and not to fire across the border unless the Mexicans intentionally shot into the American onlookers and their property, the mission was frustrating. The army could do little more than make formal protest and try to control the movement of civilians north of the border. As General [Tasker H.] Bliss pointed out in 1913, he could not guarantee anyone's safety until either the Mexicans stopped fighting or he occupied the Mexican border towns and created a buffer zone south of the Rio Grande. The other phase of the army's duties, preventing battles north of the border, was even more thankless. The traditional Anglo-Mexican hostility among the border citizens was stimulated by the revolution and complicated by the fact that some Anglo and Mexican groups wanted either to provoke a military intervention or to aid one or another of the revolutionary factions. Ordinary crimes masqueraded as revolutionary activity. Civilian law enforcement was confused and often ineffective, since Anglo peace officers became increasingly trigger-happy, vigilantism flourished, and Mexican-American constables

and judges were paralyzed by their fear of persecuting their *companeros*.[10]

By 1914, Wilson was overtly supporting Carranza. In April of that year, after Huerta's forces arrested American sailors in Tampico, Mexico, US forces landed at Veracruz to cut off Huerta's support. However, Wilson's occupation of Veracruz nearly miscarried when Mexicans protested the violation of their sovereignty. According to historian Lynn V. Foster, the plan "almost united all of Mexico behind Huerta," and "forced even Carranza and Zapata to denounce the invasion."[11] By mid-summer though, forces loyal to Carranza defeated Huerta and forced him into exile. With Huerta gone, US forces evacuated Veracruz in November 1914.

Unfortunately for Mexico and the United States, the carnage continued, this time on an even greater scale. Before Carranza could establish complete dominance in Mexico, forces loyal to Villa and Zapata assailed him. Along the Rio Grande, Brigadier General James Parker and his 1st Cavalry Brigade were ordered to secure the border. "His three cavalry regiments," wrote Millett, "were given a nine-hundred-mile border to patrol and protect, and he thought that the restrictions placed on his men were odious. Scattered into sixteen different posts and more than thirty outposts, his forces could only react and chase, leaving the initiative to the bandits."[12] While Wilson vacillated, supporting neither side, the Mexican Revolution spilled across the border.

Major General Frederick Funston and the Plan of San Diego

The Plan of San Diego was first discovered by a deputy sheriff from Hidalgo County, Texas, in January 1915. Having arrested Brasilio Ramos Jr., the deputy found documents in the man's possession that called for a Mexican-American insurrection and race war on the border. It was thought that the plan had originated in San Diego, Texas. It called for Mexicans and Mexican-Americans to take back all territory lost by Mexico at the end of the Mexican-American War. The plan also called for blacks, Indians, and Japanese-Americans to join with the Mexican-Americans in killing all male Anglos above the age of 16.[13]

At first, Government officials were skeptical and generally believed the plan was nothing more than a "hysterical fantasy."[14] Texas Governor James G. Ferguson and US Army Major General Frederick Funston, the new Commander of the Southern Department, also believed the plan dubious at best.[15] In fact, a Federal judge in Brownsville, Texas, released one of the San Diego plotters, telling the man, "You ought to be tried for lunacy, not for conspiracy against the United States."[16] Soon, however, as word spread about the planned race war, panicky whites in the lower Rio

Grande were clamoring for increased security. In response to the growing concern, the Governor sent additional Texas Rangers to the lower Rio Grande, while Funston increased US Army patrols. Millett believes that "Funston was not enthusiastic about army peacekeeping, but he hoped that it would calm the civilians and he thought that his troopers would be more effective than the Texas militia the governor might send."[17]

In early April 1915, a portion of Villa's army assaulted Carranza's forces in Matamoros only to be defeated. The attack brought the Mexican Revolution to America's door and increased nervousness along the border. Shortly after his defeat in Matamoros, Villa's forces were again defeated at the Battle of Celaya where they were driven west, giving Carranza's army complete control of the lower Rio Grande. Nevertheless, as the fighting died down between Villa and Carranza, raids into Texas increased markedly.[18]

There had always been a certain amount of cross-border criminal activity in the lower Rio Grande, but in May 1915, the raids into Texas suddenly increased. With the new attacks came an increase in violence as well as many new targets.[19] The chief sponsors of the new attacks were two Mexican-Americans, Luis de la Rosa and Aniceto Pizana. Both were key operatives within the Plan of San Diego movement. In fact, according to James A. Sandos, "Handbills proclaiming De la Rosa Chief of Operations and Pizana Chief of Staff circulated along both sides of the border and incited all Mexicans to rise."[20] It had taken both men some time to organize their guerrilla movement, but by early summer, they were striking into Texas with 25 to 100 followers determined to carry out the Plan of San Diego.[21]

In May, Rosa and Pizana launched sweeping raids into Texas. Millett wrote that "the turmoil in the lower valley reached epidemic proportions for civil authorities were receiving almost daily reports of a bandit gang robbing outlying farms and ranches of arms, horses, cows, equipment, and food."[22] Fully supplied by their initial raids, the "de la Rosa group," as Funston called them, launched new and more deadly guerrilla attacks in July. In these new raids, the Plan of Diego promoters vandalized stores, destroyed railroad bridges, and killed at least two Texans.[23] Sandos notes that the de la Rosa group "attacked symbols of change in the valley such as equipment associated with the railroad, telegraph, automobile and irrigation; and visited reprisals on Mexicans and Tejanos who helped Americans."[24]

With only 20,000 US Army soldiers to guard a 2,000-mile border, Major General Funston was hard pressed from the start.[25] (See map 5.)

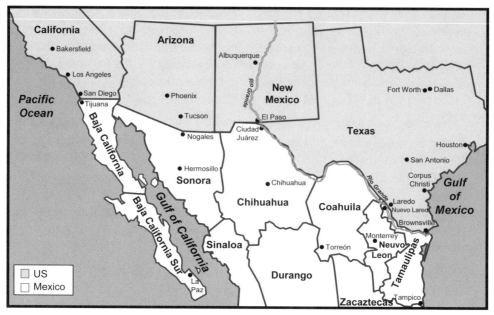

Map 5. The 2,000-Mile US-Mexican Border.

The top commanders soon realized that it would be nearly impossible to stop small raiding parties from penetrating across the border. According to US Army historian Andrew J. Birtle, Funston "responded to the crisis by spreading his troops out in penny packets in an effort to protect every small community. In doing so, he overextended his forces to such an extent that many outposts were too weak either to defend themselves or to hunt the bandits aggressively."[26] To make matters worse, Washington refused to give Funston permission to cross into Mexico, even under the doctrine of hot pursuit.[27]

By late summer, Funston was convinced that Carranza was supporting the insurgents. He was certain the attacks had a "fixed purpose and design to invade our territory, promote strife, and make war upon our people."[28] The Mexican press inflamed the situation by endorsing and promoting the Plan of San Diego while a few of Carranza's generals openly supplied the revolutionaries. Birtle points out that the insurgents were even "occasionally led by Carrancista officers."[29] It has been suggested by some historians that Carranza used the Plan of San Diego plotters to his own advantage, hoping the attacks would pressure President Wilson into full diplomatic recognition of his regime.[30] According to historians Charles H. Harris and Louis R. Sadler, "Carranza emerges as a master manipulator, as in his use of Mexican-Americans as pawns. The only times the Plan functioned were when it received support from Mexico, and such support was only forthcoming when it suited Carranza's purposes. Viewing Mexican-Americans as a fifth column, Carranza skillfully played on their hopes and fears as a means of exerting pressure on the United States."[31] By late summer, Carranza's plan was clearly having the desired effect.

For the US Army, the situation deteriorated further when Texas Rangers and vigilantes began killing Mexican-Americans they suspected of involvement in the raids. In what by now had become a familiar theme along the border, Texas Rangers inflamed the situation and further complicated the mission of the US Army. On 8 August, after a practically violent attack by 60 raiders on property associated with the King Ranch, the Texas Rangers struck back. According to an account in David Montejano's *Anglos and Mexicans in the Making of Texas, 1836–1986*, "the Rangers began a systematic manhunt and killed 102 Mexicans; citizens and army officers who saw the bodies, however, estimated that at least 300 Mexicans were killed."[32] Millett further illuminates the atrocities, writing:

> The hardware stores quickly sold out their firearms, vigilance committees were formed, and a reign of terror, led by the Texas Rangers and local police officers, began against the Mexican-American population. Bullet-riddled bodies of Mexican men and boys appeared along the roads, and piles of 'bandits' were photographed beside mass graves. Mexican refugees fled across the river into Tamaulipas, abandoning their property in Texas to Anglo confiscators.[33]

The Washington Post expressed outrage with the ongoing chaos and demanded that the US Army take charge of the border:

> It is high time that control of the border should be assumed by the United States Army. In view of the danger of involving the two countries through the mischievous and ignorant activity of local officers, the wonder is that the government did not from the first perform its duty of taking control of the border. The situation at present does not permit the thought that deputy sheriffs and their posses are capable of exercising the discretion required. They see only the incident before them, and have no sense of responsibility to the country.[34]

While Funston adamantly refused to perform civil duties in the lower Rio Grande Valley, he did call for reinforcements. One of the units sent to the border was the 26th Infantry Regiment from the 2d Division, commanded by Colonel Robert L. Bullard. Arriving in Brownsville on 15 August, Bullard assembled the rest of his command, which included three cavalry squadrons and two batteries of field artillery. Once again, however, there were simply not enough soldiers. "Given an area one hundred miles along the Rio Grande and one hundred and fifty into the interior," Millett wrote, "Bullard's troops could not patrol and protect all the towns. Despite the fact that both the Twenty-Sixth Infantry and the cavalry had small detachments scattered all over the lower valley and patrolled actively, some of the raiders punched through the cordon."[35] Indeed, the infusion of US Army reinforcements seemed to do little to stop the raids. As Harris and Sadler point out in their article "The Plan of San Diego and the Mexican-United States War Crisis of 1916: A Reexamination":

> The situation in the Lower Valley was critical by mid-September. More than half of the army's mobile units had been concentrated between Laredo and Brownsville, but the presence of these additional troops did not deter the guerrillas, who continued to cross in ever-increasing numbers. On September 13, marauders attacked a patrol camped on the Rio Grande, killing two cavalrymen and wounding two others. Eleven days later, some eighty raiders led by a Carrancista officer crossed by boat near Progreso, where they looted and burned a store, killed one soldier, and wounded two. As the Mexicans withdrew across the river, several hundred Carranza soldiers provided covering fire. An American soldier captured during this foray was taken across the river, executed, and his head displayed on a pike by the raiders.[36]

The campaign on the border in 1915 proved both vexing and deadly for the US Army. Funston, so infuriated by the raids, recommended summary executions for captured raiders, a request quickly denied by the War Department. In all, 17 soldiers were wounded, and 11 lost their lives.[37] In the end, the situation was stabilized, albeit not by the Army but by President Wilson.

On 14 October, the Wilson Administration granted Carranza's soldiers the use of American railroads to expedite the transport of troops through Laredo and Eagle Pass. The action enabled the reinforcements to help defeat Villa's attack on Agua Prieta. On 19 October, in another gesture of goodwill, Wilson recognized Carranza's government. While there were certainly numerous reasons for recognizing Carranza's regime, Sandos notes, "a legitimate government in Mexico, could be held accountable for regional unrest while an unrecognized faction could not. From the U.S. perspective, recognition of a Mexican Government meant identifying a responsible authority that could provide border security." Not surprisingly, within 1 week the border raids ceased.[38]

Pershing's Expedition and the Return of the Plan of San Diego Plotters

Unfortunately, Wilson's support for Carranza came at a price. Villa was outraged by Wilson's support for Carranza and was determined to strike back at the United States. In the aftermath of his defeat at Agua Prieta, however, Villa's army had been greatly reduced, forcing him to revert to more unconventional means of warfare. On 9 January 1916, Villa's guerrillas attacked a train carrying American miners and engineers near Chihuahua City, Mexico. As 16 Americans were pulled from the train and executed, a Villista officer shouted, "Tell Wilson to come and save you, and tell Carranza to give you protection."[39]

Villa's attack on the American miners and engineers was merely a precursor to his new campaign against the United States. On the morning of 9 March 1916, Villa and approximately 500 of his soldiers attacked the town of Columbus, New Mexico. In the ensuing melee, the Mexicans looted the town before being driven off by US Army soldiers from the 13th Cavalry Regiment. By the time the smoke cleared, 17 Americans and nearly 100 raiders were dead.[40] "All over the United States," wrote Clendenen, "there was an immediate demand for the prompt punishment of the raiders."[41]

When Secretary of War Newton D. Baker ordered Army Chief of Staff Hugh L. Scott to go after Villa, Scott asked, "Do you want to make war on one man? Suppose Villa should get on the train and go to Guatemala, Yucatan or South America: are you going after him?" It was Baker's first day as Secretary of War and he quickly agreed with Scott. New orders were drawn up and sent to Funston: "You will promptly organize an adequate military force of troops from your department under the command of Brigadier General John J. Pershing and will direct him to proceed promptly across the border *in pursuit of the Mexican band which attacked the town of Columbus*, New Mexico, and the troops there on the morning of the ninth instant."[42] Funston agreed wholeheartedly with the order and suggested that "unless Villa is relentlessly pursued and his forces scattered he will continue raids. . . . If we fritter away the whole command guarding towns, ranches and railroads it will accomplish nothing if he can find refuge across the line after every raid." Clearly, Funston and the US Army learned a valuable lesson from the 1915 raids.[43]

According to Sandos, President Wilson issued "two distinct messages. To the American interventionists he pledged capture [of Villa], while at the same time he limited his field commander to dispersal." To make sure there was no misunderstanding, Wilson, through the War Department, issued the following order to Funston on 13 March: "The President desires that your attention be especially and earnestly called to his determination that the expedition into Mexico is *limited* to the purposes originally stated, namely *the pursuit and dispersion of the band or bands that attacked Columbus, N. M. . . .*[44]

In mid-March, Pershing started moving his forces across the border into the Mexican State of Chihuahua. In all, 12,000 US Army soldiers participated in Pershing's expedition. The Army penetrated several hundred miles into Mexico during the year-long campaign, and although they failed to capture Villa, they managed to disrupt Villa's brigands and prevent further attacks into the United States.[45] Secretary of War Baker later remarked:

> The expedition was in no sense punitive, but rather defensive. Its objective, of course, was the capture of Villa if that could be accomplished, but its real purpose was an extension of power of the United States into a country disturbed beyond control of the constituted authorities of the Republic of Mexico, as a means of controlling lawless aggregations of bandits and preventing attacks by them across the international frontier. This purpose it fully and finally accomplished.[46]

The greatest threat to the United States associated with Pershing's expedition came not from Villa but from the reorganized Plan of San Diego members. While Carranza was outraged by the US incursion, he did not support the new attacks by the Plan of San Diego members. Unfortunately for the United States, rogue elements within his army provided certain levels of support.[47]

Taking full advantage of Pershing's expedition into Mexico, de la Rosa and his Plan of San Diego adherents began conducting new raids into Texas. Two large raids on the towns of Glenn Springs and Boquillas, Texas, in early May left two US soldiers dead. Convinced that the Plan of San Diego followers were responsible, Major General Funston immediately called for reinforcements, asking for the mobilization of the Arizona, New Mexico, and Texas National Guards. Wilson and his Administration agreed with Funston's request, and on 9 May, the units were federalized and sent to the border.[48]

Unlike 1915, the new Plan of San Diego attacks provoked a far different response from the US Army. Much to their shock and amazement, the raiders were pursued back into Mexico by the US Army. These hot pursuits proved quite successful, often resulting in the killing of raiders and the return of hostages. However, by June, the raids had not stopped, forcing President Wilson to federalize all National Guard forces in the United States. Once mobilized, they, too, were sent directly to the border.[49]

As these new forces began to make their presence felt, Wilson ordered a halt to all US Army border crossings. Knowing full well that the United States might be drawn into the war in Europe, Wilson was determined to bring the crisis on the border to a close. Trying to avoid all-out war with the United States, Carranza was equally resolute to end the volatile situation. As the US Army abandoned its cross-border pursuits, Carranza's forces rounded up the Plan of San Diego members. De la Rosa himself was eventually apprehended and placed under house arrest, although the Mexican Government refused a request for his extradition. In January 1917, after lengthy negotiations, Pershing's expeditionary force was finally withdrawn from Mexican soil. Within 4 months of Pershing's withdrawal, the United States declared war on Germany, ushering in America's participation in World War I.[50]

While the American public was extremely disappointed in the US Army's failure to capture Villa, it was pleased with the restored stability along the border.[51] As with all US Army incursions into Mexico, the events of 1915–17 inflamed the Mexican population. Sandos points out that the events "worked to embitter Mexican relations with the United States for more than twenty years. . . ."[52] However, the emergence of the United States onto the world stage in 1917 had a calming effect on Mexico. As Fehrenbach states, "The 'North American question' had been and was destined to be Mexicans' overriding external problem, and when the United States turned outward toward the world, the predominant feeling was always relief in Mexico."[53] Although the US Army continued to perform limited missions on the Mexican border for the rest of the 20th century, nothing equaled the strife and conflict of those turbulent years.

Summary

Like the border missions conducted in 1850s and 1870s, the US Army in the early 20th century found that inert defensive positions and patrolling alone could not prevent hostile bands from crossing the border and wrecking havoc on the United States. Military officers in the early 1900s realized, as did their predecessors, that the best tactical response was to launch counterraids and hot pursuits across the border. Once the political decision was made permitting the US Army to cross the border, the raids decreased significantly. Reminiscent of the particulars concerning Diaz in the 1870s, the US Army and US Government ultimately persuaded Carranza to police his own border, thereby ending the proliferation of raids into the United States.

Notes

1. Lynn V. Foster, *A Brief History of Mexico* (New York: Facts on File, Inc., 1997), 138.

2. T. R. Fehrenbach, *Fire and Blood: A History of Mexico* (New York: Da Capo Press, 1995), 453; Foster, 146.

3. Robert E. Quirk, *The Mexican Revolution, 1914–1915* (New York: W. W. Norton & Company, Inc., 1960), 1–2.

4. David Montejano, *Anglos and Mexicans in the Making of Texas, 1836–1986* (Austin: University of Texas Press, 1987), 82.

5. Ibid., 83.

6. Timothy J. Dunn, *The Militarization of the U.S.-Mexico Border, 1978–1992: Low-Intensity Conflict Doctrine Comes Home* (Austin: The Center for Mexican-American Studies and the University of Texas, 1996), 8.

7. Fehrenbach, 491.

8. Clarence C. Clendenen, *Blood on the Border: The United States Army and the Mexican Irregulars* (London: The Macmillan Company, 1969), 145–146, 150.

9. Ibid., 153.

10. Allan R. Millett, *The General: Robert L. Bullard and Officership in the United States Army, 1881–1925* (Westport, CT: Greenwood Press, 1975), 275–276.

11. Foster, 164; John S. D. Eisenhower, *Intervention! The United States and the Mexican Revolution, 1913–1917* (New York: W. W. Norton & Company, 1993), 127.

12. Millett, 276.

13. Ibid., 277; Charles H. Harris and Louis R. Sadler, "The Plan of San Diego and the Mexican-United States War Crisis of 1916: A Reexamination," *The Hispanic American Historical Review*, Vol. 58, No. 3 (August 1978), 381; Eisenhower, 212.

14. Millett, 277.

15. Ibid.

16. Clendenen, 181.

17. Millett, 277.

18. Clendenen, 179–180.

19. Ibid, 180; Eisenhower, 212.

20. James A. Sandos, "Pancho Villa and American Security: Woodrow Wilson's Mexican Diplomacy Reconsidered," *Journal of Latin American Studies*, Vol. 13, No. 2 (November 1981), 296.

21. Millett, 277.

22. Ibid.

23. Ibid.

24. James A. Sandos, *Rebellion in the Borderlands: Anarchism and the Plan of San Diego, 1901–1923* (Norman: University of Oklahoma Press, 1992), 188.

25. Eisenhower, 211.

26. Andrew J. Birtle, *U. S. Army Counterinsurgency and Contingency Operations Doctrine, 1860–1941* (Washington DC: Center of Military History, United States Army, 2004), 200.

27. Clendenen, 183.

28. Eisenhower, 211.

29. Birtle, 199–200.

30. Ibid., 199.

31. Harris and Sadler, 405–406.

32. Montejano, 119.

33. Millett, 278.

34. *The Washington Post*, 9 September 1915.

35. Millett, 279.

36. Harris and Sadler, 389. See also, "Mutilated by Raiders," *The Washington Post*, 1 October 1915.

37. Birtle, 200; Harris and Sadler, 390.

38. Sandos, "Pancho Villa and American Security," 298.

39. Eileen Welsome, *The General and the Jaguar: Pershing's Hunt for Pancho Villa: A True Story of Revolution and Revenge* (New York: Little, Brown and Company, 2006), 66.

40. Birtle, 201; Eisenhower, 217.

41. Clendenen, 213.

42. Eisenhower, 230 (italics in the original).

43. "General Funston to the Adjutant General, March 10, 1916," *Papers Relating to the Foreign Relations of the United States With the Address of the President to Congress, December 5, 1916*, University of Wisconsin Digital Collection, 482–483.

44. Sandos, "Pancho Villa and American Security," 301 (italics in the original).

45. Birtle, 202.

46. Sandos, "Pancho Villa and American Security," 310.

47. Clendenen, 215; Sandos, "Pancho Villa and American Security," 305.

48. Sandos, "Pancho Villa and American Security," 304; Clendenen, 287.

49. Clendenen, 289; Sandos, "Pancho Villa and American Security," 305–306; Thomas A. Bruscino Jr. "A Troubled Past: The Army and Security on the Mexican Border, 1915–1917," Unpublished Article, 18.

50. Sandos, "Pancho Villa and American Security," 305; Bruscino, 19–20.

51. Sandos, "Pancho Villa and American Security," 310–311.

52. Ibid., 311.

53. Fehrenbach, 527.

Chapter 5

The US Army and Mexican Border Security, 1919–Present

> With the military looking for a new job, a more easily accomplished mission for existing forces would be patrolling the borders. It is, of course, absurd that the most powerful nation on earth cannot prevent a swarming land invasion by unarmed Mexican peasants. The U.S. Army is entirely capable of plugging the holes permanently, and border duty would be excellent military training.
>
> Former US Army Officer, *Newsday*, 17 September 1991

> Violence along the U.S.-Mexico border is undergoing what U.S. law-enforcement authorities call 'an unprecedented surge.'
>
> *The Washington Times*, 9 March 2007

> The military does not appear to have a direct legislative mandate to protect or patrol the border or to engage in immigration enforcement.
>
> Congressional Research Service, 23 May 2006

> President Bush proposed using up to 6,000 National Guard members on a rotational basis for up to a year to support the U.S. Border Patrol as it recruits and trains more members.
>
> American Forces Information Service, 24 May 2006

Deployment of US Army Forces on the Mexican Border and the Battle of Juarez, 1919

By the end of World War I, the US-Mexican border remained dangerous and volatile as Mexican President Venustiano Carranza continued his battle to subdue Francisco "Pancho" Villa. Attacks by bandits and would-be revolutionaries were still common in 1919, which forced the US Army to take up positions once again along the border. By spring 1919, approximately 18,500 US Army soldiers (6,000 cavalry, 8,500 infantry, and 4,000 artillery) were positioned either on the border or within easy striking distance. This force also included 9 squadrons of US Army aviation units and 10 balloon companies. Cavalry and infantry regiments were stationed from Nogales, Arizona, to Ringgold, Texas, and were supported by machine-gun battalions, a brigade of artillery, numerous motor transport companies, and a sizable allotment of engineers.[1]

In June 1919, Villa again made his presence felt by moving 4,000 of his soldiers to the outskirts of Juarez, Mexico, threatening to capture the city from Federal forces. Employing all manner of subterfuge, Villa's lieutenants managed to smuggle ammunition to their guerrilla forces from across the border in El Paso.[2] Sensing Villa might launch an attack on Juarez, Brigadier General James B. Erwin, the Commander of the El Paso Military District, requested additional troops for his sector. In no time, the 2d Cavalry Brigade, commanded by Colonel Selah R. H. "Tommy" Tompkins, took up positions east of El Paso, while the 4th Battalion, 24th Infantry Regiment, and a battalion of the 82d Artillery Regiment assumed positions in the streets of downtown El Paso.[3]

On 14 June, Villa attacked Federal troops in Juarez. The Federal commander, General Francisco Gonzalez, put up only token resistance and fell back to Fort Hidalgo northwest of town. With the withdrawal of the Federal soldiers, Villa positioned his forces in the center of Juarez, while a large contingent occupied the racetrack southeast of the city. The following night, Villa's forces, firing from rooftops in Juarez, shot several soldiers and civilians in El Paso. Outraged, Erwin responded by ordering 25 US Army snipers into position to return fire. Next, Erwin ordered his artillery to fire on the racetrack. As the indirect fire fell on the revolutionaries in and around the racetrack, the black soldiers of the 24th Infantry raced across the international bridge into Juarez, chasing Villa's command out of the town and vigorously pursuing the panic-stricken forces as they fled south.[4]

In conjunction with the attack of the 24th Infantry, Colonel Tompkins's cavalry forces, consisting of elements from the 7th and 5th Cavalry Regiments as well as a battalion of the 82d Artillery, crossed the Rio Grande at three fording sites east of El Paso. According to the *Los Angeles Times* reporter at the scene, "There were approximately 3,600 American troops on Mexican soil ten minutes after they were ordered to make the crossing."[5]

At a hastily convened press conference, Erwin told reporters that "because of the wounding of several innocent and law-abiding persons residing in El Paso and the wounding of two United States soldiers . . . under the authority given me . . . from the headquarters of the Southern Department, June 12, 1919, I ordered troops of my command to cross the border and disperse the Villistas. But, upon no account, were they to undertake an invasion of Mexico."[6]

The next morning, Tompkins caught up with Villa's command near Zaragoza, Mexico, called artillery fire onto Villa's position, and launched his attack. In what writer Leon C. Metz describes as "the last great cavalry charge in American history," Tompkins routed Villa's soldiers from the field. After pursuing him and his command for 15 miles, Tompkins and his horse soldiers returned to El Paso.[7]

The US Army's response to the crisis in Juarez was quick and decisive. When shots were fired into El Paso, wounding American soldiers and civilians, the Army swiftly crossed into Mexico with overwhelming firepower and drove Villa's revolutionaries away from the border. Once again, the Mexicans were outraged by the US Army's blatant cross-border attack. The incident forced high-ranking US Government officials to assure Mexico that the assault on Juarez was not a full-blown invasion and was designed to merely protect American citizens. Regardless of Mexican denunciations, the US Army's actions in Juarez had the desired effect. There would be no more problems with Villa, who soon withdrew from the border.[8] After the Battle of Juarez, approximately 20,000 US Army soldiers continued to guard the Mexican border. However, many high-ranking Government officials believed still more troops were needed. On 20 June, Secretary of War Newton C. Baker appeared before the Military Affairs Committee of Congress and recommended "at least 100,000 soldiers . . . be available at all times to deal with the Mexican menace."[9] Baker's plan was rejected, and by 1922, Congress reduced the size of the Regular Army to less than 150,000 soldiers.[10]

Although reduced in strength, the US Army continued to patrol the Mexican border. In 1920, a reporter from *The New York Times* observed the workings of the 5th Cavalry Regiment in the Big Bend, Texas, area. "Twice a day every foot of the border line is patrolled by cavalrymen and infantrymen," he reported. He also noted that US Army airplanes patrolled the entire area up to three times a day. With increased political stability in Mexico, however, the US Army border commands faced little trouble.[11] As an example, in 1923, Lucian K. Truscott, a young officer assigned to Camp Marfa in Presidio County, Texas, reported that "bandits were still active occasionally in northern Mexico during this period, but their raiding across the border had been uncommon for some years, except for occasional cattle rustling."[12]

By the 1920s, the US Army's prominent role in combating armed raiders and revolutionaries from south of the border came to a close. "As the 20th century progressed," suggests Graham H. Turbiville Jr., "border law enforcement became more regularized in dealing with cross-border criminality and border control generally."[13] As new Federal agencies stepped forward to help state and local law enforcement police the border, the US Army's commitment diminished greatly.

Immigration Issues and Operation WETBACK

During the 1920s, immigration issues took center stage along the border as the US Government attempted to regulate the flow of Mexican immigrants into the country. Writer Timothy J. Dunn points out that "it was characterized by the application of what [James D.] Cockcroft has termed the 'revolving door' immigration policy of alternating periods of large-scale immigration and massive deportation." To help regulate this policy, the US Government established the US Border Patrol in 1924.[14]

During the 1930s, the revolving door policy continued. With America's entry into World War II and the ensuing severe labor shortage that followed, the US Government reached an agreement with the Mexican Government to allow farm workers into the United States on a temporary basis. Called the *Bracero* Program, the accord brought thousands of impoverished Mexicans across the border. By the early 1950s, however, the Immigration and Naturalization Service (INS) grew increasingly alarmed by the massive influx of undocumented Mexican workers, a situation that threatened to undermine the capabilities of the Border Patrol.[15]

In 1954, US Attorney General Herbert Brownell launched Operation WETBACK, a major coordinated effort to round up and expel illegal aliens. Hoping to reinforce the Border Patrol, Brownell turned to the US Army for help. To his dismay, the proposal was rejected. The Army claimed such an operation would "seriously disrupt training programs at a time when the administration's economy slashes were forcing the service to drastically cut its strength. Army generals also opposed the idea because a division would be needed just to begin to control the influx, while sealing off the border would require even more troops." General Joseph Swing thought placing US Army soldiers on the border was "a perfectly horrible" idea that would "'destroy' relations with Mexico."[16]

There were also other reasons to reject the plan. In a State Department dispatch from Robert C. Goodwin to Secretary of Labor James Mitchell, Goodwin called attention to a cartoon from Mexico's largest newspaper. In his book *Operation Wetback: The Mass Deportation of Mexican Undocumented Workers in 1954*, Juan Ramon Garcia wrote that "the cartoon portrayed a terror-stricken Mexican with his back to the wall and a huge bayonet marked 'U.S. Troops' pointed at his chest, with the legend 'Between the Sword and the Wall.'" Goodwin suggested that "if the Army proposal were to be followed, we (the United States) would get a similar reaction from a rather large group in this country."[17] A US Embassy counselor in Mexico wrote that Mexicans believed the US Army would be used in the deportation effort:

The slant of these comments, which are being overheard in typical local cafes, restaurants, and other like places patronized by Mexicans, is that we are imperialistic, war-mongering and ruthless people and that the poor and wretched wetbacks who want to return to the lands which the United States forcibly took from Mexico, will be met by a hail of American bullets.[18]

In the end, the Border Patrol conducted the operation, rounding up and deporting more than 100,000 Mexicans. According to Dunn, Mexicans were not the only ones humiliated by Operation WETBACK. "Mexican Americans were also negatively affected, because the operation graphically reinforced the principle of their having to be prepared at all times to prove their U.S. citizenship or face deportation."[19] It was perhaps a wise decision on the part of the US Army to avoid participating in Operation WETBACK.

The US Army and Mexican Border Security, 1982–2005

By the early 1980s, the geography of the border had changed markedly. While still containing vast open areas of deserts and mountains, urbanization had greatly transformed its topography. Heavily populated twin border communities propelled by farming, tourism, and steady gains in production made their mark on the region. By 1995, the border population reached 10.6 million. However, there were still major problems. At the forefront was the continuing influx of illegal aliens and the explosion in drug smuggling.[20]

The recommitment of US Army forces to the Mexican border began gradually in the early 1980s with the passage of the Defense Authorization Act of 1982. To help the military assist law enforcement in the War on Drugs, the act relaxed certain rules pertaining to the Posse Comitatus Act.[21] Under the heading "Military Cooperation With Civilian Law Enforcement Officials," the new law allowed the military to operate and maintain military equipment on loan to Federal law enforcement agencies, train law enforcement officers, and report and share information on criminal activity. According to Dunn:

During the 1980s the military was called on to take a new and expanding role in antidrug efforts in the border region, one which centered on providing high-tech equipment and conducting surveillance operations and training exercises. The Defense Department was apparently slated to become extra 'eyes and ears' for civilian agencies engaged in drug enforcement activities and, at least on occasion, in playing this role it also aided immigration enforcement efforts on the border.[22]

It should be noted that while this new statutory exception to the Posse Comitatus Act greatly enhanced the military's capabilities in the War on Drugs, it did not allow Active-Duty military personnel to directly participate in law enforcement activities.[23]

By the mid-1980s, illegal drugs were still pouring across the Mexican border, prompting a massive response from Federal law enforcement. In 1986, the US Government launched Operation ALLIANCE to help stem the flow of illegal drugs from Mexico. The United States military played a key role in this endeavor, helping with airborne surveillance, equipment loans, and training. In 1989, as the War on Drugs heated up, a new act further expanded the military's role in law enforcement. The 1989 Defense Authorization Act allowed the military to lend equipment to state and local law enforcement as well as foreign law enforcement units involved in the War on Drugs. The new law also allowed the US military to operate its own equipment for the campaign.

In 1989, Joint Task Force-Six (JTF-6) was established to further assist in President George H. W. Bush's War on Drugs. The new headquarters element "was established to serve as the planning and coordinating operational headquarters to support local, state, and Federal law enforcement agencies within the Southwest border region to counter the flow of illegal drugs into the United States. JTF-6's original area of operations consisted of the four border states of California, Arizona, New Mexico and Texas—a land area of more than 660,000 square miles."[24]

Along with the formation of JTF-6, the Secretary of Defense declared the War on Drugs a "high-priority national security mission." The Pentagon promptly responded to the new "high-priority" mission, sending both Active and Reserve personnel to the border. US military support to local law enforcement quickly expanded. According to Dunn:

> [The new missions] . . . took myriad forms in the U.S.-Mexico border region. These included conducting small-unit and long-range reconnaissance patrols in hard-to-cover areas; providing, deploying, and monitoring electronic ground sensors, providing intelligence support; clearing brush and improving roads along the border; training law enforcement personnel in intelligence analysis and survival skills; providing air transport of law enforcement personnel in interdiction and eradication efforts; staffing listening and observation posts; using remotely piloted

reconnaissance aircraft; staging military exercises in suspected drug trafficking zones; conducting radar and imaging missions; providing operational planning assistance and providing DOD personnel to develop data bases as well as mapping and reconnaissance folders for Border Patrol sectors.[25]

With US military forces committed to so many missions along the border, it was only a matter of time before they encountered Mexican criminal elements. On 13 December 1989, 50 Active-Duty Marines conducting a training exercise with the Border Patrol near Nogales, Arizona, stumbled onto a gang of Mexican drug smugglers. When the horse-mounted smugglers fled, the Marines sent up a flare and were immediately fired on by the Mexicans. In response, a Border Patrol agent ordered the Marines to return fire. Although no one was injured in the ensuing gun battle, the Marine flare started a fire that eventually burned 300 acres of a federally protected forest. According to Dunn, "These were the first recorded shots fired by active-duty military personnel on the border in drug enforcement activity." He concluded that "this episode escalated the level of confrontation on the border between smugglers and law enforcement officials and was a dramatic departure from past practices, although subsequently the military purposefully sought to avoid such armed clashes."[26]

Additional laws were passed by Congress in the early 1990s to strengthen the military's role in the ongoing drug war. Dunn points out that these new laws "pulled the military farther [sic] into the domestic front of the War on Drugs, effectively relaxing the Posse Comitatus restrictions even more. It specifically mandated that the military conduct training exercises 'to the maximum extent practicable' in drug-interdiction areas in which smuggling into the United States occurred or was believed to have occurred. This definition clearly implicated the U.S.-Mexico border region."[27]

The US Army continued to support the War on Drugs along the border throughout the 1990s. However, many groups in the United States and Mexico were extremely critical of the mission. While various Government agencies supported the Border Patrol, it was US military involvement that sparked the greatest protest. In an article for *Military Review*, Turbiville points out that, all through the 1990s, "US Active and Reserve Component military support to drug enforcement along the border has sparked protest in the United States and from Mexican official and media sources. Charges that the border is being 'militarized' became increasingly common in the mid-1990s."[28]

Several high-profile incidents brought the protest to a fever pitch. In January 1997, a soldier from the 5th US Special Forces Group shot and wounded a Mexican drug smuggler near Brownsville, Texas, after the smuggler fired on his observation post.[29] In May, a Marine patrol shot and killed Ezequiel Hernandez Jr., an American citizen living near Redford, Texas. Apparently, the Marine mistook Hernandez's recreational target practice for hostile fire. According to a reporter from *The Washington Post*, the incident "cast a pall over the role of the U.S. military in supporting federal anti-drug efforts along the border. Immediately after the shooting the military's El Paso-based Joint Task Force 6, which deploys small teams of troopers to help spot traffickers in border areas, suspended operations in the sector. . . ."[30] By July, Secretary of Defense William Cohen suspended the use of armed soldiers on the border and, according to the *Chicago Tribune*, "ordered an end to routine use of ground troops for anti-drug missions."[31]

As JTF-6 dealt with the public relations fallout from the shootings, the Government Accounting Office reported that the Border Patrol's effectiveness in stemming the tide of illegal immigration over the last 4 years was at best inconclusive. The report suggested that their "measures have shifted many illegal crossings away from the urban centers . . . into more remote areas."[32] In December 1997, retired Army General Barry McCaffrey, the Clinton Administration's new drug policy adviser warned, "the U.S. Border Patrol must triple its size to 20,000 agents if it is going to take control of the 2,000-mile untamed border with Mexico."[33] Again, as the US Army had found during its long history on the border, limited manpower, static defensive positions, and simple patrolling measures could not thwart individuals or groups determined to cross the border.

In 1999, Secretary of Defense Cohen announced a new policy for the employment of the military in the antidrug campaign along the border. "Under the new policy, armed troops may be deployed only with specific permission of the secretary of defense or his deputy," the Pentagon announced. From 1989 to 1997, JTF-6 performed 799 antidrug missions with ground troops. Cohen wanted to ensure that, in the future, "all the counter-drug activities receive the appropriate level of oversight."[34]

After the terrorist attacks on 11 September 2001, the US military's role in supporting law enforcement agencies along the Mexican border greatly increased. In 2004, JTF-6 was renamed Joint Task Force North (JTF North), and its missions expanded to include homeland security support to all Federal law enforcement agencies. From its headquarters at Biggs Army Airfield, Fort Bliss, Texas, JTF North today is involved in a myriad of Federal law enforcement support missions. According to its website:

> JTF North is the Department of Defense organization tasked to support our nation's federal law enforcement agencies in the identification and interdiction of suspected transnational threats within and along the approaches to the continental United States. Transnational threats are those activities conducted by individuals or groups that involve international terrorism, narcotrafficking, alien smuggling, weapons of mass destruction, and includes the delivery systems for such weapons that threaten the national security of the United States.[35]

In the past, JTF North received requests from Federal law enforcement agencies for support and matched them with Active and Reserve units who volunteered for support missions. According to the JTF North website, "Once a unit volunteers JTF North facilitates mission planning and execution with the unit and supported agency. In accordance with Department of Defense policy, missions must have a training value to the unit or provide a significant contribution to national security."[36] A list of JTF North's four support categories include the following:

Operational Support
Aviation Support Operations
Aviation Transportation/Insertion/Extraction
Aviation Medical Evacuation (MEDEVAC)
Aviation Reconnaissance
Daytime Operations
Nighttime Operations
Air and Maritime Surveillance Radar (Secretary of
    Defense is the approval authority)
Unmanned Aircraft Systems (UAS)
Ground Surveillance Radar
Listening Post/Observation Post (Secretary of Defense is
    the approval authority)
Ground Sensor Operations
Ground Transportation

Intelligence Support
LEA [Law Enforcement Agency] Case Sensitive
    Intelligence Support
Collaborative Threat Assessment

Geospatial Intelligence Support
Modified Threat Vulnerability Assessment
Threat Link Analysis Product

Engineering Support
Personnel Barriers
Vehicle Barriers
Lights
Roads
Bridges

General Support
Mobile Training Teams
Basic Marksmanship
Combat First Aid/Trauma Training
Counterdrug Investigation Course
Counterdrug Marksman/Observer Training Course
Counterdrug Narco-Terrorism Personal Protection
Counterdrug Special Reaction Team Training
Drug Trafficking Organization Targeting
Integrated Mission Planning
Intelligence and Link Analysis
Interview and Interrogation
Law Enforcement Interdiction of Narcotics
Multi-Subject Tactical Instruction
Threat Assessment Training
Other training as requested
Tunnel Detection
Transportation
Sustainment[37]

A mission performed by the 1st Squadron, 6th Air Cavalry Regiment, 1st Combat Aviation Brigade, 1st Infantry Division, in March 2007 provides a good example of current operations conducted by JTF North and volunteer units on the border. The 1-6 CAV performed air surveillance and night reconnaissance missions to support the Border Patrol. According to an agent with the Border Patrol, the mission was requested from JTF North "to assist in the interdiction of narcotrafficking and alien smuggling along the U.S. and Mexican border. The 1-6 CAV provided us with aircraft and manpower to fly in certain areas of southern New Mexico. They were our eyes and our ears. They were able to communicate with our agents on the ground in the event they observed any illegal activity." By the end of the mission, 1-6 CAV helped the Border Patrol arrest 182 illegal immigrants and an unknown quantity of illegal drugs. "This is just another front on the 'Global War on Terrorism,'" the Commander of 1-6 CAV, Lieutenant Colonel John Thompson, remarked.[38]

Engineering efforts by JTF North and volunteer units supporting border security have also been impressive. From 1989 to 1998, engineer support missions were responsible for 536.6 miles of road construction and improvements. Engineers also placed 7 miles of lighting, 31 miles of border fence, and 15 miles of vehicle barriers. Since 1999, JTF North and volunteer engineer units have added 82 miles of road construction and improvements, 12.3 miles of perimeter lighting, 12.5 miles of fence, and 20 miles of vehicle barriers.[39]

Unfortunately, these efforts have done little to stem the tide of illegal immigrants or curtail an upsurge in criminal activity. As border governors and outraged citizens demanded action, President George W. Bush ordered 6,000 National Guard troops to the border on 15 May 2006. Operation JUMP START calls for National Guard Soldiers to be used as a stopgap measure until the Border Patrol can train 6,000 new agents. The Congressional Research Service reports that "the Guard will assist the Border Patrol by operating surveillance systems, analyzing intelligence, installing fences and vehicle barriers, building roads, and providing training. Guard units will not be involved in direct law-enforcement activities and will be under the control of the Governors."[40] The Chief of the National Guard Bureau, Lieutenant General H. Steven Blum, made clear to reporters "that the National Guard's mission at the border is not a military one, but is military support to civil authorities. It's important that people in Mexico don't see this mission as a closure of the border to legal immigration, trade and business."[41]

A large percentage of the National Guard troops were sent to the border area near Nogales, Arizona, considered by many to be one of the most difficult areas to police. Dennis Steele, a writer for *Army Magazine*, reported that "scores of illegals trickled across in broad daylight from Nogales, Mexico (the border divides the towns), and hundreds dashed across every night."[42] By August 2006, Guard Soldiers from various states were hard at work performing engineering tasks and administrative duties, while others in the Nogales area were assigned to static observation posts along the border. Steele points out that "no Guard members are acting in a direct law enforcement capacity; they do not pursue or arrest suspected illegal immigrants or smugglers. Guard soldiers manning isolated observation posts, which are stand-off points located 100 to 500 yards or more from the border, have small arms to protect themselves, but this mission calls for them to avoid confrontation."[43] While most National Guard Soldiers serve on the border with their units for 21-day deployments, others volunteer to fill "duration" positions or sign up for 90-day to 2-year assignments.[44] No one can predict whether Operation JUMP START will have a significant impact on the current border situation, but like Major Bennet Riley's soldiers in 1829, the US Army continues to watch the Mexican border.

Notes

1. Robert B. Armstrong, "Big Force on Border," *Los Angeles Times*, 1 June 1919.

2. Leon C. Metz, *Border: The U.S.-Mexico Line* (El Paso, TX: Mangan Books, 1989), 230.

3. Ibid., 231; "American Guns Fire on Villa," *Los Angeles Times*, 16 June 1919.

4. Metz, 231; "American Guns Fire on Villa."

5. "American Guns Fire on Villa."

6. Ibid.

7. Metz, 231.

8. "Explaining to Mexico," *Los Angeles Times*, 17 June 1919; Metz, 232.

9. Arthur Sears Henning, "Calls 26,450 Volunteers To Serve on Border," *Chicago Daily Tribune*, 21 June 1919.

10. Richard W. Stewart, general ed., *American Military History*, Vol. 2, *The United States Army in a Global Era, 1917–2003*, Army Historical Series (Washington, DC: Center of Military History, United States Army, 2005), 59.

11. "Ready for War in the Big Bend of Texas," *The New York Times*, 25 January 1920.

12. Lucian K. Truscott Jr., *The Twilight of the U.S. Cavalry: Life in the Old Army, 1917–1942* (Lawrence: University Press of Kansas, 1989), 56, 58.

13. Graham H. Turbiville Jr., "US-Mexican Border Security: Civil-Military Cooperation," *Military Review*, July–August 1999, 3.

14. Timothy J. Dunn, *The Militarization of the U.S.-Mexico Border 1978–1992* (Austin, TX: The Center for Mexican-American Studies, 1996), 11. See also, James D. Cockcroft, *Outlaws in the Promised Land: Mexican Immigrant Workers and America's Future* (New York: Grove Press), 1986.

15. Dunn, 13–14.

16. Juan Ramon Garcia, *Operation Wetback: The Mass Deportation of Mexican Undocumented Workers in 1954* (Westport, CT: Greenwood Press, 1980), 169, 171.

17. Ibid., 169.

18. Ibid., 170.

19. Dunn, 17.

20. "The International Boundary and Water Commission, Its Mission, Organization and Procedures for Solution of Boundary and Water Problems," *International Boundary and Water Commission*, 2, http://www.ibwc.state.gov/html/about_us.html

21. For a brief history of the Posse Comitatus Act, see Matt Matthews, *The Posse Comitatus Act and the United States Army: A Historical Perspective* (Fort Leavenworth, KS: Combat Studies Institute Press, 2006).

22. Dunn, 111.

23. Ibid., 106, 107.

24. "Joint Task Force North Originally Established in 1989," Joint Task Force North History, http://www.jtfn.northcom.mil/subpages/history.html

25. Dunn, 124.

26. Ibid., 130–131.

27. Ibid., 119.

28. Turbiville, 1.

29. James Pinkerton, "GI Shoots Suspect at Mexican Border Observation Post," *Houston Chronicle*, 28 January 1997.

30. William Branigin, "Questions on Military Role Fighting Drugs Ricochet From a Deadly Shot," *The Washington Post*, 22 June 1997.

31. Douglas Holt, "Pentagon Halts Routine Use of Troops for Anti-Drug Border Patrols," *Chicago Tribune*, 28 January 1999.

32. William Branigin, "Border Control Strategy Difficult to Assess; Billions Spent," *The Washington Post*, 15 December 1997.

33. "Nation in Brief War on Drugs Mexican Border Patrol Too Small, Adviser Says," *The Atlanta Journal-Constitution*, 6 December 1997.

34. Holt.

35. Joint Task Force North Mission, http://www.jtfn.northcom.mil/subpages/mission.html

36. Joint Task Force North Homeland Security Support, http://jtfn.northcom.mil/subpages/hmland_sec_sppt.html

37. Ibid.

38. Major Deanna Bague, US Northern Command-Newsroom, 28 March 2007, http://www.northcom.mil/newsroom/news_release/2007/032807.html

39. "JTF North Homeland Security Support," *Fact Sheet Joint Task Force North*, Fact Sheet Number 3, 23 March 2007.

40. Stephen R. Vina, "Border Security and Military Support: Legal Authorizations and Restrictions," *CRS Report for Congress*, 23 May 2006.

41. Sergeant Sara Wood, "Guard Border Mission 'Right Way To Do Business,' Chief Says," *American Forces Press Service*, 2, http://www.ngb.army.mil/news/archives/080906-SWB_right_way.aspx

42. Dennis Steele, "Operation Jump Start: National Guard Aids Border Patrol Mission," *Army Magazine*, November 2006, 19, 31.

43. Ibid., 31.

44. Ibid.

Conclusions

The history of the US Army's security mission on the Mexican border is one of distinguished service under the most difficult conditions. Since Brevet Major Bennet Riley's march to the Mexican border in 1829, relations between the two nations have run the gamut from mutual concord and harmony to enmity and all-out war. The annexation of Texas and the subsequent operations of Brigadier General Zachary Taylor's Army of Observation and Army of Occupation exacerbated Mexican animosity toward the United States. The ramifications of this conflict still incite anger among many Mexicans. From 1846 to the early 20th century, the Army's role on the southern border was intimately tied to the westward expansion of America. Obviously, that era will not repeat itself, but certain themes still resonate today that affect the US Army's role along the Nation's southern border.

One of those themes is the recurring use of military operations to protect US citizens and property along the border against various threats by a variety of military means. With the close of the Mexican War, the US Army was called on to secure the immense border. Between 1848 and 1917, the Army performed this mission, for the most part, by stationing small numbers of troops along the border in small outposts and patrolling the area to discourage cross-border banditry, Indian movements, and criminal activities of all kinds. The US Army found it could not adequately protect the new territory against incursions and raids with the limited manpower at its disposal. The distances were too great and the terrain to difficult given the paucity of troops committed to the mission. The Army also discovered that maintaining static defensive positions and simple patrolling measures could not stop determined adversaries from breaching the border, a conundrum that continues to this day.

Alternating with the use of outposts and patrols, the Army frequently conducted cross-border attacks to preempt or retaliate against various groups. The use of such operations depended on the degree of internal Mexican Government stability and its ability to control its own border regions—a second persistent theme in the story of the US Army on the border. With the end of the American Civil War, the US Army's actions from 1865 to 1867 in tacit support of liberal forces against Maximilian and the French in Mexico helped restore much of the goodwill that had been lost in the aftermath of the Mexican War. Major General Philip Sheridan's intrepid moves along the US-Mexican border not only helped to oust a major European power from the US southern border but also helped for a time to restore and stabilize the Mexican Government.

Always undermanned, the US Army again found that immobile defensive positions and sparse patrolling of the immense border region could not possibly stop border incursions when instability returned to the border region in the 1870s and 1880s. Most often, swift cross-border strikes on enemy sanctuaries by the US Army or major police actions by the Mexican Army on its side of the border were the only viable means of stopping cross-border raids. While US Army raids across the border ultimately proved successful, they rekindled Mexican hostility toward the United States. The most notable among these many cross-border operations by the Army was the 1916–17 Pershing expedition that sought to destroy Pancho Villa's forces that had been conducting attacks on US territory.

After World War I, the United States still stationed nearly 20,000 Army troops along the border to defeat a still undeterred Villa who captured the Mexican city of Juarez in June 1919 and appeared ready to attack the US city of El Paso. The last cross-border attack by the US Army took place on 12 June 1919 as soldiers under the command of US Brigadier General James Erwin attacked Villa's base and drove him out of Juarez. Villa never again posed a threat to the border. By the 1920s, the direct military role of the Army in securing the Nation's southern border came to an end. Instead of the US Army preventing raids and launching punitive expeditions, for the next 60 years, the Nation confronted the large-scale immigration of Mexicans to the United States, which began in the 1920s and continued after World War II. When directed to secure the border, the Army leadership was typically unenthusiastic. For example, it was particularly forceful and successful in objecting to being tasked to participate in the expulsion of illegal Mexican immigrants in the mid-1950s during Operation WETBACK. By the 1950s, the Army had come full circle from its active participation along the border between 1846 and 1919 due to the nonmilitary nature of the illegal immigration problem and to its greatly expanded worldwide commitments during the Cold War.

In the early 1980s, the Army was ordered to participate in the War on Drugs, and again, it proved a reluctant player in that mission. Prohibited by the Posse Comitatus Act from taking a direct role in combating drug traffickers, the Army (and other elements of the US Armed Forces) instead was tasked to provide various types of logistics, intelligence, equipment, and training support to civilian law enforcement agencies. The recommitment of military personnel to the Mexican border in the early 1980s proved highly controversial on both sides of the border and did little to restrict the deluge of drugs or illegal immigrants. The killing of an American citizen by a Marine patrolling the border in 1997 added to the growing controversy and forced the Federal Government to curtail the "routine use of ground troops for anti-drug missions."[*] In spite of the broad support provided by the military, the Border Patrol's manpower was too limited to produce dramatic results.

A third recurring theme in the Army's history on the border is the practical working and legal relationship between US military forces and Federal, state, and local agencies involved in securing the border. While the US Army has provided broad support to Federal law enforcement agencies tasked with guarding the Nation's southern border, its missions have been constrained by Federal law. Soldiers are strictly limited to a supporting role; they cannot make arrests. The post-9/11 use of the Army, primarily the National Guard, to reinforce and support civilian agencies along the border in their antidrug and anti-illegal immigration efforts appears to be more successful than earlier efforts because of better integration, policy guidance, and the willingness to cooperate on all sides. The provision of certain Army technical expertise and equipment to civilian agencies and the assumption of civilian support duties by the Army National Guard to free border agents for more active roles appear to be effective in recent years. Unless additional exceptions are added to the Posse Comitatus Act or policymakers scrap the law, the Army will continue to be limited to a supporting role. The events since 9/11, however, have added a new dimension to the border security issue. With the renewed threat of international terrorism, it may well behoove policymakers to reexamine the provisions and interpretations of the Posse Comitatus Act in light of today's security needs.

While the historical record shows that the US military is capable of performing innumerable types of missions, its presence on the US-Mexican border is domestically and internationally contentious, as policymakers are certainly aware. The Army's role on the border today no longer includes active patrolling or combat operations. Army support to civilian law enforcement agencies can be expected to continue and perhaps to increase in the coming years. The historical record also demonstrates, however, that the solution to securing the Nation's southern border is ultimately a political solution involving domestic US and domestic Mexican politics and US-Mexican diplomatic relations.

---

[*]Douglas Holt, "Pentagon Halts Routine Use of Troops for Anti-Drug Border Patrols," *Chicago Tribune*, 28 January 1999.

Bibliography

Published Articles

Bancroft, Frederic. "The French in Mexico and the Monroe Doctrine." *Political Science Quarterly*, Vol. 11, No. 1, March 1896.

Barker, Nancy Nichols. "France, Austria, and the Mexican Venture, 1861–1864." *French Historical Studies*, Vol. 3, No. 2, Autumn 1963.

Barker, Nancy N. "Monarchy in Mexico: Harebrained Scheme or Well-Considered Prospect?" *The Journal of Modern History*, Vol. 48, No. 1, March 1976.

Bourne, Edward G. "The United States and Mexico, 1847–1848." *The American Historical Review*, Vol. 5, No. 3, April 1900.

Frazer, Robert W. "Maximilian's Propaganda Activities in the United States, 1865–1866." *The Hispanic American Historical Review*, Vol. 24, No. 1, February 1944.

"Frontier Region of Mexico: Notes to Accompany a Map of the Frontier." *Geographical Review*, Vol. 3, No. 1, January 1917.

Gordon, Leonard. "Lincoln and Juarez—A Brief Reassessment of Their Relationship." *The Hispanic American Historical Review*, Vol. 48, No. 1, February 1968.

Hanna, Kathryn Abbey. "The Roles of the South in the French Intervention in Mexico." *The Journal of Southern History*, Vol. 20, No. 1, February 1954.

Harris, Charles H., and Louis R. Sadler. "The Plan of San Diego and the Mexican-United States War Crisis of 1916: A Reexamination." *The Hispanic American Historical Review*, Vol. 58, No. 3, August 1978.

Hoskins, Halford L. "French Views of the Monroe Doctrine and the Mexican Expedition." *The Hispanic American Historical Review*, Vol. 4, No. 4, November 1921.

Jore, Jeff. "Pershing's Mission in Mexico: Logistics and Preparation for the War in Europe." *Military Affairs*, Vol. 52, No. 3, July 1988.

Lofgren, Charles A. "Force and Diplomacy, 1846–1848: The View From Washington." *Military Affairs*, Vol. 31, No. 2, Summer 1967.

McCornack, Richard Blaine. "James Watson Webb and French Withdrawal From Mexico." *The Hispanic American Historical Review*, Vol. 31, No. 2, May 1951.

Miller, Robert Ryal. "Matias Romero: Mexican Minister to the United States During the Juarez-Maximilian Era." *The Hispanic American Historical Review*, Vol. 45, No. 2, May 1965.

Morrison, Michael A. "Martin Van Buren, the Democracy, and the Partisan Politics of Texas Annexation." *The Journal of Southern History*, Vol. 61, No. 4, November 1995.

Sandos, James A. "Pancho Villa and American Security: Woodrow Wilson's Mexican Diplomacy Reconsidered." *Journal of Latin American Studies*, Vol. 13, No, 2, November 1981.

Scott, James Brown. "The American Punitive Expedition Into Mexico." *The American Journal of International Law*, Vol. 10, No. 2, April 1916.

Steele, Dennis. "Operation Jump Start: National Guard Aids Border Patrol Mission." *Army Magazine*, November 2006.

Turbiville, Graham H. "US-Mexican Border Security: Civil-Military Cooperation, *Military Review*, July–August 1999.

Unpublished Article

Bruscino, Thomas A. Jr. "A Troubled Past: The Army and Security on the Mexican Border, 1915–1917.

Books

Adams, Anton. *The War in Mexico*. Chicago: The Emperor's Press, 1998.

Anderson, Gary Clayton. *The Conquest of Texas: Ethnic Cleansing in the Promised Land, 1820–1875*. Norman: University of Oklahoma Press, 2005.

Arnold, James R. *Jeff Davis's Own: Cavalry, Comanches, and the Battle for the Texas Frontier*. New York: John Wiley & Sons, Inc., 2000.

Baguley, David. *Napoleon III and His Regime: An Extravaganza*. Baton Rouge: Louisiana State University Press, 2000.

Bauer, K. Jack. *The Mexican War, 1846–1848*. New York: Macmillan Publishing Company, Inc., 1974.

_____. *Zachary Taylor: Soldier, Planter, Statesman of the Old Southwest*. Baton Rouge: Louisiana State University Press, 1985.

Beers, Henry Putney. *The Western Military Frontier, 1815–1846*. Philadelphia: Porcupine Press, 1975.

Bemis, Samuel Flagg. *John Quincy Adams and the Foundations of American Foreign Policy*. New York: Alfred A. Knopf, 1949.

Birtle, Andrew J. *U.S. Army Counterinsurgency and Contingency Operations Doctrine, 1860–1941*. Washington, DC: Center of Military History, United States Army, 2004.

Blackmar, Frank W. *Kansas: A Cyclopedia of State History, Embracing Events, Institutions, Industries, Counties, Cites, Towns, Prominent Persons, etc.* Chicago: Standard Publishing Company, 1912.

Brackett, Albert G. *History of the United States Cavalry, From the Formation of the Federal Government to the 1st of June, 1863*. New York: Greenwood Press Publishers, 1968.

Brenner, Anita. *The Wind That Swept Mexico: The History of the Mexican Revolution, 1910–1942*. Austin: University of Texas Press, 1996.

Callcott, Wilfrid Hardy. *Liberalism in Mexico, 1857–1929*. Stanford: Stanford University Press, 1931.

_____. *Santa Anna: The Story of an Enigma Who Once Was Mexico*. Norman: University of Oklahoma Press, 1936.

Carlson, Paul H. *"Pecos Bill:" A Military Biography of William R. Shafter*. College Station: Texas A&M University Press, 1989.

Chitwood, Oliver Perry. *John Tyler Champion of the Old South*. Newtown, CT: American Biography Press, 1990.

Christensen, Carol, and Thomas Christensen. *The U.S.-Mexican War*, San Francisco: Bay Books, 1998.

Chynoweth, W. Harris. *The Fall of Maximilian*. London: By the Author, 1872.

Clendenen, Clarence C. *Blood on the Border: The United States Army and the Mexican Irregulars*. London: The Macmillan Company, 1969.

Cockcroft, James D. *Outlaws in the Promised Land: Mexican Immigrant Workers and America's Future*. New York: Grove Press, 1986.

Cooke, Philip St. George. *Scenes and Adventures in the Army, or Romance of Military Life*. Philadelphia: Lindsay and Blakiston, 1857.

Corti, Count Egon Caesar. *Maximilian and Charlotte of Mexico*. Vol. 2. Translated by Catherine Alison Phillips. New York: Alfred A. Knopf, 1928.

Cunningham, Michele. *Mexico and the Foreign Policy of Napoleon III*. Gordonsville, VA: Palgrave Macmillan, 2000.

Dary, David. *The Santa Fe Trail: Its History, Legends, and Lore*. New York: Alfred A. Knopf, 2000.

Doubler, Michael D. *Civilian in Peace, Soldier in War: The Army National Guard, 1636–2000*. Lawrence: University Press of Kansas, 2003.

Dunn, Timothy J. *The Militarization of the U.S.-Mexico Border, 1978-1992: Low-Intensity Conflict Doctrine Comes Home*. Austin: The Center for Mexican-American Studies and the University of Texas, 1996.

Eisenhower, John S. D. *Intervention! The United States and the Mexican Revolution, 1913–1917*. New York: W. W. Norton & Company, 1993.

_____. *So Far From God: The U.S. War With Mexico, 1846–1848*. New York: Random House, 1989.

Fehrenbach, T. R. *Fire and Blood: A History of Mexico*. New York: Da Capo Press, 1995.

Ferrell, Robert H., ed. *Monterrey Is Ours! The Mexican War Letters of Lieutenant Dana, 1845–1847*. Lexington: The University Press of Kentucky, 1990.

Foos, Paul. *A Short, Offhand, Killing Affair: Soldiers and Social Conflict During the Mexican-American War*. Chapel Hill: The University of North Carolina Press, 2002.

Foster, Lynn V. *A Brief History of Mexico*. New York: Facts on File, Inc, 1997.

Garcia, Juan Ramon. *Operation Wetback: The Mass Deportation of Mexican Undocumented Workers in 1954*. Westport, CT: Greenwood Press, 1980.

Goetzmann, William H. *Army Exploration in the American West, 1803–1863*. Lincoln and London: University of Nebraska Press, 1979.

Grant, U. S. *Personal Memoirs of U. S. Grant*. Edited by E. B. Long. Cleveland, OH, and New York: The World Publishing Company, 1952.

Haley, Edward P. *Revolution and Intervention: The Diplomacy of Taft and Wilson With Mexico, 1910–1917*. Cambridge, MA: The MIT Press, 1970.

Hamilton, Holman. *Zachary Taylor: Soldier of the Republic*. Indianapolis, IN: The Bobbs-Merrill Company, 1941.

Harris, Charles H. III, and Louis R. Sadler. *The Texas Rangers and the Mexican Revolution*. Albuquerque: University of New Mexico Press, 2004.

Heidler, David S., and Jeanne T. Heidler. *The Mexican War*. Westport, CT: Greenwood Press, 2006.

Howes, Kelly King. *Mexican American War*, Detroit, MI: The Gale Group, Inc., 2003.

James, Daniel. *Mexico and the Americans*. New York: Frederick A. Praeger, 1963.

Johnson, William Weber. *Heroic Mexico: The Violent Emergence of a Modern Nation*. Garden City, NY: Doubleday and Company, Inc., 1968.

Katz, Friedrich. *The Secret War in Mexico: Europe, the United States and the Mexican Revolution*. Chicago: The University of Chicago Press, 1981.

Kaufmann, J. E. and H. W. Kaufmann. *Fortress America: The Forts That Defended America, 1600 to the Present*. Cambridge, MA: Da Capo Press, 2004.

Leckie, William H., with Shirley A. Leckie. *The Buffalo Soldiers: A Narrative of the Black Cavalry in the West*. Revised Edition. Norman: University of Oklahoma Press, 2003.

Leiker, James N. *Racial Borders: Black Soldiers Along the Rio Grande*. College Station: Texas A&M University Press, 2002.

Leon, Arnoldo De. *They Called Them Greasers. Anglo Attitudes Toward Mexicans in Texas, 1821–1900*. Austin: University of Texas Press, 1983.

Mahin, Dean B. *One War at a Time: The International Dimensions of the American Civil War*. Washington, DC: Brassey's, 1999.

Mahon, John K. *History of the Militia and the National Guard*. New York: Macmillan Publishing Company, 1983.

Manning, William R. *Early Diplomatic Relations Between the United States and Mexico*. "The Albert Shaw Lectures on Diplomatic History, 1913." New York: Greenwood Press Publishers, 1968.

Marszalek, John F. *Sherman: A Soldiers Passion for Order*. New York: Vintage Books, 1994.

Matthews, Matt. *The Posse Comitatus Act and the United States Army: A Historical Perspective*. Fort Leavenworth, KS: Combat Studies Institute Press, 2006.

May, Robert E. *Manifest Destiny's Underworld: Filibustering in Antebellum America*. Chapel Hill and London: The University of North Carolina Press, 2002.

McAfee, Ward, and J. Cordell Robinson. *Origins of the Mexican War: A Documentary Source Book*. Vol. 1. *U.S. Relations With Latin American Nations*. Salisbury, NC: Documentary Publications, 1982.

McCormac, Eugene Irving. *James K. Polk: A Political Biography to the Prelude of War, 1795–1845*. Newtown, CT: American Political Biography Press, 1995.

Merrill, James M. *Spurs to Glory: The Story of the United States Cavalry*. Chicago: Rand McNally and Company, 1966.

Metz, Leon C. *Border: The U.S.-Mexico Line*. El Paso, TX: Mangan Books, 1989.

Millett, Allan R. *The General: Robert L. Bullard and Officership in the United States Army, 1881–1925*. Westport, CT: Greenwood Press, 1975.

Montejano, David. *Anglos and Mexicans in the Making of Texas, 1836–1986*. Austin: University of Texas Press, 1987.

Moseley, Edward H., and Paul C. Clark Jr. *Historical Dictionary of the United States-Mexican War*. Lanham, MD, and London: The Scarecrow Press, Inc., 1997.

Nagel, Paul C. *John Quincy Adams, a Public Life, a Private Life*. New York: Alfred A. Knopf, 1998.

Nance, Joseph Milton. *After San Jacinto: The Texas-Mexican Frontier, 1836–1841*. Austin: University of Texas Press, 1963.

Nevins, Joseph. *Operation Gatekeeper: The Rise of the "Illegal Alien" and the Making of the U.S.-Mexico Boundary*. New York: Routledge, 2002.

Nofi, Albert A. *The Alamo and the Texas War for Independence*. New York: De Capo, 1994.

O'Connor, Richard. *Sheridan the Inevitable*. Indianapolis, IN: The Bobbs-Merrill Company, Inc., 1953.

Oliva, Leo E. *Soldiers on the Santa Fe Trail*. Norman: University of Oklahoma Press, 1967.

Pierce, Michael D. *The Most Promising Young Officer: The Life of Ranald Slidell Mackenzie*. Norman and London: University of Oklahoma Press, 1993.

Pitner, Ernst. *Maximilian's Lieutenant: A Personal History of the Mexican Campaign, 1864–7*. Translated and Edited by Gordon Etherington-Smith. Albuquerque: University of New Mexico Press, 1993.

Pletcher, David M. *The Diplomacy of Annexation: Texas, Oregon, and the Mexican War*. Columbia: University of Missouri Press, 1973.

Prucha, Francis Paul. *A Guide to the Military Posts of the United States, 1789–1895*. Madison: The State Historical Society of Wisconsin, 1964.

Quirk, Robert E. *The Mexican Revolution, 1914–1915*. New York: W. W. Norton and Company Inc., 1960.

Ridley, Jasper. *Maximilian and Juarez*. New York: Ticknor & Fields, 1992.

Rister, Carl Coke. *Border Command: General Phil Sheridan in the West*. Norman: University of Oklahoma Press, 1944.

Roeder, Ralph. *Juarez and His Mexico*. Vols. 1 and 2. New York: The Viking Press, 1947.

Rosenbaum, Robert J. *Mexicano Resistance in the Southwest: "The Sacred Right of Self-Preservation."* Austin: University of Texas Press, 1981.

Sandos, James A. *Rebellion in the Borderlands: Anarchism and the Plan of San Diego, 1901–1923*. Norman: University of Oklahoma Press, 1992.

Schulz, Donald E. *Mexico and the Future*. Carlisle, PA: Strategic Studies Institute, US Army War College, 1995.

Sheridan, Philip H. *Personal Memoirs of P. H. Sheridan*, Vol. 2. North Scituate, MA: Digital Scanning, Inc., 1999.

Sherman, William Tecumseh. *Memoirs of General W. T. Sherman*. New York: The Library of America, 1990.

Sides, Joseph C. *Fort Brown Historical: History of Fort Brown, Texas Border Post on the Rio Grande*. San Antonio, TX: The Naylor Company, 1942.

Simon, John Y., ed. *The Papers of Ulysses S. Grant*. Vols. 15, 16. Carbondale: Southern Illinois University Press, 1988.

Simpson, Colonel Harold B. *Cry Comanche: The 2nd U.S. Cavalry in Texas, 1855–1961*. Hillsboro: TX: Hill Junior College Press, 1979.

Smart, Charles Allen. *Viva Juarez! A Biography*. Philadelphia: J. B. Lippincott Company, 1963.

Smith, Thomas Tyree. *Fort Inge: Sharps, Spurs and Sabers on the Texas Frontier, 1849–1869*. Austin, TX: Eakin Press, 1993.

Stewart, Richard W. general ed. *American Military History*. Volume 2. *The United States Army in a Global Era, 1917–2003*. Army Historical Series. Washington, DC: Center of Military History, United States Army, 2005.

Thomas, David Yancey. *A History of Military Government in Newly Acquired Territory of the United States*. New York: The Columbia University Press, 1904.

Toulmin, Harry Aubrey. *With Pershing in Mexico*. Harrisburg, PA: The Military Service Publishing Company, 1935.

Truscott, Lucian K. Jr. *The Twilight of the U.S. Cavalry: Life in the Old Army, 1917–1942*. Lawrence: University Press of Kansas, 1989.

Uglow, Loyd M. *Standing in the Gap: Army Outposts, Picket Stations, and the Pacification of the Texas Frontier, 1866–1886*. Fort Worth, TX: Christian University Press, 2002.

Ulibarri, Richard O. *American Interest in the Spanish Southwest, 1803–1848*. San Francisco: R&E Research Associates, 1974.

Utley, Robert M. *Frontier Regulars: The United States Army and the Indian, 1866–1891*. New York: Macmillan Publishing Company, Inc., 1973.

_____. *Lone Star Justice: The First Century of the Texas Rangers*. Oxford: Oxford University Press, 2002.

Vandiver, Frank E. *Black Jack: The Life and Times of John J. Pershing*. College Station: Texas A&M University Press, 1977.

Webb, Walter Prescott. *The Texas Rangers: A Century of Frontier Defense*. Austin: University of Texas Press, 1996.

Weber, David J. *The Mexican Frontier, 1821–1846: The American Southwest Under Mexico*. Albuquerque: University of New Mexico Press, 1982.

Weems, John Edward. *To Conquer a Peace*. College Station: Texas A&M University Press, 1974.

Weigley, Russell F. *History of the United States Army*. Bloomington: Indiana University Press, 1984.

Welsome, Eileen. *The General and the Jaguar: Pershing's Hunt for Pancho Villa: A True Story of Revolution and Revenge*. New York: Little, Brown and Company, 2006.

Winders, Richard Bruce. *Crisis in the Southwest: The United States, Mexico, and the Struggle Over Texas*. Wilmington, DE: SR Books, 2002.

Wooster, Robert. *Soldiers, Sutlers, and Settlers: Garrison Life on the Texas Frontier*. College Station: Texas A&M University Press, 1987.

Young, Elliott. *Catarino Garza's Revolution on the Texas-Mexico Border*. Durham, NC, and London: Duke University Press, 2004.

Young, Otis E. *The First Military Escort on the Santa Fe Trail, 1829, From the Journal and Reports of Major Bennet Riley and Lieutenant Philip St. George Cooke*. Glendale, CA: The Arthur H. Clark Company, 1952.

Internet Sources

Blue Skyways, Kansas State Library. Chouteau's Island. http://skyway.lib.ks.us/history/chouteau.html

"The International Boundary and Water Commission, Its Mission, Organization and Procedures for Solution of Boundary and Water Problems." *International Boundary and Water Commission*, 2. http://www.ibwc.state.gov/html/about_us.html

Joint Task Force North History. http://www.jtfn.northcom.mil/subpages/history.html

Joint Task Force North Homeland Security Support. http://www.jtfn.northcom.mil/subpages/hmland_sec_sppt.html

Joint Task Force North Mission. http://www.jtfn.northcom.mil/subpages/mission.html

U.S. Northern Command-Newsroom. 28 March 2007. http://www.northcom.mil/newsroom/news_release/2007/032807.html

Wood, Sergeant Sara. "Guard Border Mission 'Right Way To Do Business,' Chief Says." American Forces Press Service. http://www.ngb.army.mil/news/archives/080906-SWB_right_way.aspx

Newspapers

"American Guns Fire on Villa." *Los Angeles Times*, 16 June 1919.

Arkansas Democrat (Little Rock, AR), 12 June 1846.

Armstrong, Robert B. "Big Force on Border." *Los Angeles Times*, 1 June 1919.

Aurora & Pennsylvania Gazette (Philadelphia, PA), 23 May 1829.

Branigin, William. "Border Control Strategy Difficult to Assess; Billions Spent." *The Washington Post*, 15 December 1997.

_____. "Questions on Military Role Fighting Drugs Ricochet From Deadly Shot." *The Washington Post*, 22 June 1997.

The Cleveland Herald (Cleveland, OH), 15 May 1846; 22 April 1846.

The Charleston Mercury (Charleston, SC), 17 October 1859.

Columbia Telescope (Columbia, SC), 7 August 1829.

Dover Gazette & Strafford Advertiser (Dover, NH), 9 May 1846.

"Explaining to Mexico." *Los Angeles Times*, 17 June 1919.

Henning, Arthur Sears. "Calls 26,450 Volunteers To Serve on Border." *Chicago Daily Tribune*, 21 June 1919.

Holt, Douglas. "Pentagon Halts Routine Use of Troops for Anti-Drug Border Patrols." *Chicago Tribune*, 28 January 1999.
Little Rock Daily Gazette (Little Rock, AR), 18 August 1865.
Louisville Public Advertiser (Louisville, KY), 19 November 1829.
The Milwaukee Journal (Milwaukee, WI), 29 January 1892.
Milwaukie Daily Sentinel (Milwaukee, WI), 6 December 1845.
Milwaukie Sentinel and Gazette (Milwaukee, WI), 1 May 1846.
"Nation in Brief War on Drugs Mexican Border Patrol Too Small, Adviser Says." *The Atlanta Journal-Constitution*, 6 December 1997.
The New York Herald, 10 December 1845; 17 December 1859.
The New-York Spectator, 1827.
New-York Spectator, 15 June 1827, 3 August 1827, 26 February 1830.
Newsday, 17 September 1991.
N. O. Picayune (New Orleans, LA), 1 November 1845
North American and United States Gazette (Philadelphia, PA), 3 February 1849.
"Official Report S. P. Heintzelman." *Daily National Intelligencer* (Washington, DC), 25 January 1860.
Pensacola Gazette (Pensacola, FL), 21 March 1846.
Pinkerton, James. "GI Shoots Suspect at Mexican Border Observation Post." *Houston Chronicle* (Houston, TX), 28 January 1997.
Raleigh Register, and North-Carolina Gazette (Raleigh, NC), 26 May 1846.
"Ready for War in the Big Bend of Texas." *The New York Times*, 25 January 1920.
"Report of Major Riley." *The New-York Spectator*, 26 February 1830.
The Scioto Gazette (Chillicothe, OH), 27 November 1845.
South Carolina Temperance Advocate and Register of Agriculture and General Literature (Columbia, SC), 23 April 1846.
The Washington Post, 9 September 1915.
Weekly Ohio Statesman (Columbus, OH), 8 October 1845.
The Weekly Raleigh Register (Raleigh, NC), 1 February 1860.

Microfilm

Taylor, Zachary. *Orders of General Zachary Taylor to the Army of Occupation in the Mexican War, 1845–1847*. Washington, DC, 1942. Combined Arms Research Library, Fort Leavenworth, KS.

Official Reports

"General Funston to the Adjutant General, March 10, 1916." *Papers Relating to the Foreign Relations of the United States With the Address of the President to Congress, December 5, 1916*. University of Wisconsin Digital Collections.
Pershing, John J. *Report of Operations of the Punitive Expedition to June 30, 1916*. Combined Arms Research Library, Fort Leavenworth, KS.

Fact Sheet

"JTF North Homeland Security Support." *Fact Sheet Joint Task Force North*. Fact Sheet Number 3, 23 March 2007.

Reports

Vina, Stephen R. "Border Security and Military Support: Legal Authorizations and Restrictions." *CRS Report for Congress*. 23 May 2006.

About the Author

Matt M. Matthews joined the Combat Studies Institute (CSI) in July 2005 after working for 16 years as a member of the World Class Opposing Force (OPFOR) for the Battle Command Training Program at Fort Leavenworth, Kansas. Mr. Matthews graduated from Kansas State University in 1986 with a B.S. in History. He served as an Infantry enlisted man in the Regular Army from 1977 to 1981, a Cavalry officer in the US Army Reserve from 1983 to 1986, and an Armor officer in the Kansas Army National Guard from 1986 to 1991. Mr. Matthews is the author of CSI Press publications *The Posse Comitatus Act and the United States Army: A Historical Perspective* and *Operation AL FAJR: A Study in Army and Marine Corps Joint Operations*. He has coauthored numerous scholarly articles on the Civil War in the Trans-Mississippi, including "Shot All to Pieces: The Battle of Lone Jack," "To Play a Bold Game: The Battle of Honey Springs," and "Better Off in Hell: The Evolution of the Kansas Red Legs." He is a frequent speaker at Civil War Roundtables, and he recently appeared on the History Channel as a historian for Bill Kurtis' *Investigating History*. Mr. Matthews has been the mayor of Ottawa, Kansas.